# THE SPLIT SOCIETY

# THE SPLIT SOCIETY

by

NICHOLAS DAVENPORT

LONDON
VICTOR GOLLANCZ LTD
1964

TO OLGA

*Printed in Great Britain by*
*The Camelot Press Ltd., London and Southampton*

# CONTENTS

# ACKNOWLEDGMENTS

ONE IS OFTEN carried along the stream of ideas blithely ignorant of the source of the many tributaries that swell the current. But I am very conscious of what came to me from the writings of Maynard Keynes. It was a great privilege to have been in direct contact with his fascinating mind in various affairs over many years.[1] And although I was an Oxford man I owe much to his Cambridge colleague Sir Hubert Henderson whom I regard as my teacher in applied economics.

Last year I became greatly indebted to Professor Brinley Thomas of Cardiff University, Mr. E. T. Jackson of the Institute of Economics and Statistics at Oxford, Mr. John Vaizey of Worcester College, Oxford, and Mr. George Ray of the National Institute of Economic and Social Research who all read the manuscript of my contributions to *The Spectator* in November 1963 on The Split Society. I am grateful also for the permission of the proprietor of *The Spectator*, Mr. Ian Gilmour, M.P., and to the present editor, Mr. Iain Macleod, M.P., for their permission to draw upon these and other of my articles in their paper. We should all be thankful that an independent weekly journal still exists which allows radical contributors to express their views without let or interference.

I am also indebted to Mr. K. G. J. C. Knowles and Mr. D. Robinson of the Oxford Institute of Economics and Statistics who were good enough to read the manuscript of the section in Part II on internal policy. None of these economists must be identified with my views which are sometimes at variance with their own. I merely want to acknowledge the great help I received from their criticism.

I am also grateful to Lady Gaitskell for allowing me to print a letter Hugh Gaitskell wrote to me on the question of the rate of interest in 1947-51.

Finally, I cannot fully express all that I owe to my wife, Olga Davenport, whose warm human understanding, lively interest in psychology and great appreciation of the arts, led me to look at the problem of a split society from a much wider angle than the economic.

[1] Apart from a journalistic contact (see p. 25) I sat with him on the board of the National Mutual Life Assurance Society.

# PART I

# POLITICAL AND ECONOMIC INTRODUCTION

ONE

# THE NATIONAL STATUS

ONE NIGHT IN January 1964 I was listening to the third programme on the radio and heard Professor Max Beloff of Oxford giving a lecture with the title "Imperial Sunset". "Within the space of a single lifetime", he said, "Britain has been transformed from being the centre and power house of a world empire into an unsuccessful candidate for admission to an embryonic federation of Western Europe." Good heavens, I thought, that was my lifetime! And my mind went back to the first moment of self-consciousness that I can remember. I was a very small child sitting on my mother's lap and I was bursting into tears on the death of Queen Victoria. This was no mark of horrible precocity, no vision of the alarming course of British history over the next sixty years. My distress was simply caused by the maid coming in to pull down the blinds, darkening the room at my mother's request to observe the national mourning. It was much later on, after I had been up at Oxford studying history and economics, that I realised that my generation had been born into a society doomed to decline —not only in outward political power but in inner strength and social cohesion. Never again would any British family pull down the blinds on the death of a reigning monarch. It would not be a significant enough event. Nor would there be any more maids in middle-class households to do it. The whole social order was passing away together with the trappings of an Empire.

It seemed to me that this was no cause for tears. Change is exciting, if it is understood, and the old order was far from perfect. In many ways it was a shocking affront to the dignity and self-respect of ordinary working people. The evolution of Great Britain into some appearance of greatness other than material world power could be the greatest blessing not only for ourselves but for the distracted world. And by a stroke of good fortune we have been given the time and the opportunity to work this out, for we no longer have to waste public funds on policing the world or for that matter on having an independent nuclear deterrent if we decide that it is useless. The Pax Americana (not forgetting the nuclear stalemate) is quite an adequate substitute for the Pax Britannica. The money that used to be squandered on the accoutrements of world power can now be more usefully spent, if we have the will, on public education, on science and technology and the much needed psychological study of human behaviour.

In our country we have enough political sense to avoid violent revolutions but from time to time the evolutionary process takes a tremendous jump. This happened early in the century when the Liberal welfare state was inaugurated by Lloyd George. Shortly after that social reformation the shattering blow of the First World War completed the disintegration of our brash, money-making, class-ridden Edwardian society. Then the Bolshevik earthquake sent tremors through the social structure of the whole western world. The revolutionary challenge to capitalist society had begun. Alas, the leaders of the British Establishment failed at that time to appreciate the extent of the social change they had to make. By stubbornly holding to outworn economic and financial policies in the late 'twenties and 'thirties they nearly brought down the British state.

About twenty years later came the counter-revolution of the fascist powers. This was the almost inevitable reaction to the force and brutality of the communist revolution but it was fostered by the fear of change and the sense of insecurity which the middle classes felt in all the European countries infected. Out of it came the Second World War, culminating in the frightful degradation of the whole human race at the hands of an insane German dictator. We British just survived thanks to indomitable national spirit and the inspired leadership of the last of the great Edwardian statesmen. But the sad record of national decline since the war is proof that the heads of the Establishment are still looking back with nostalgia to the days of our world surpemacy and failing to adjust their thinking to the changed world status of the nation. Why can they not see that it could become a much more honourable status than it was in the days of the great colonial epoch?

Churchill remarked when the war was over that he did not see himself as Prime Minister presiding over the liquidation of the British Empire. But this was precisely the sort of Prime

Minister we wanted—if the liquidation could be carried through with the imagination, the spirit and the panache of a Churchill. Attlee began well with the grant of immediate freedom to India but he failed to see that without India we could not remain a colonial power for a minute longer. India had sustained the Empire with its man-power. When India had gone Imperialism had to be liquidated. What was necessary there and then was a declaration of the right of self-determination extended to all our colonial people. If Attlee had been more imaginative he might have set up a Ministry of De-Colonialisation to help the people prepare for the day of their liberation by training their civil servants, educating their future leaders at our universities and perhaps drilling and disciplining their military men and their very necessary Praetorian guards. He might have called a London conference to work out the time-table for the Colonial trains to independence, fast and slow as the case might be. Imagine the world acclaim of the new greatness of Great Britain if a Prime Minister had had the imagination to denounce colonialism before the communists did!

But even the Labour leaders after the war were clinging to the past. They were so imbued with the traditions of the British Commonwealth—especially Labour party traditions in the great Dominions of the old Empire—that they turned their backs on the new Europe. I remember calling on Dalton in Strasbourg in 1950. It was plain to everyone there that the leader of the British delegation did not take the European assembly at all seriously. He had an official chauffeur and each time he got into his car he and the chauffeur intoned a hymn of hate against the Germans. It was the year when the Germans for the first time had been invited to Strasbourg as good Europeans. Yet, as Lord Boothby has reminded us in his fascinating autobiography, European leadership at that time was ours for the asking. The reputation of British parliamentary democracy and socialism stood high in Europe. The British Labour movement, having avoided the extremism of Continental Marxist-socialism, had survived and Europe was at last ready to follow its example of moderation. But Europe got the cold shoulder from British Labour leaders.

It was typical of the lack of imagination of the Conservative caucus in 1951 that they never thought of enlisting the services of such an able and enlightened European as Boothby who had the right vision of the European future. I cannot imagine that if Boothby had been Foreign Secretary in 1963 we would have suffered such national humiliation as when the innocent Macmillan came suppliant to De Gaulle at the door of a United Europe and was snubbed for his pains.

But that is the nature of the British Establishment of today. Like most other Establishments it becomes stuffy and stuck. It refuses to receive new ideas or employ unconventional men. It is the burden of this book to show how and why it became stuck, economically and financially, in the nineteen-twenties and thirties—the fateful years of economic crisis which bred the great disasters of our time.

"Looking back", said Professor Carstairs in the Reith Lectures, 1962, "it now seems that our concept of ourselves as a nation and people reached a peak of naïve self-esteem in late Victorian times, a heady altitude from which we have been descending ever since. . . . Formerly our attitude to the rest of the world was outward looking. We annexed, administered and developed large areas and sent missionaries to convert their peoples to our religion in the conviction that we were doing all this for their own good as well as ours. Then gradually this tide turned. We found it less easy to be quite sure that our way of life was necessarily the best."

Our elder generation are clearly perplexed by the destruction of their old spiritual values. Although unwilling to accept the communist view of a mechanistic, God-less universe they have acquired no new faith to replace their old Christian beliefs. Meanwhile many of our teenagers run wild like savages, which is apparently a sign of boredom, an inability to feel integrated with society as a whole. The long hair and the fantastic clothes are a somewhat pathetic, if spirited, attempt to lead a creative, individualistic life instead of a mechanistic "admass" life. All this wonderful physical and nervous force could be diverted into something more useful for the human race if only the Establishment knew how. The skills and ebullience of "Mods" and "Rockers" might be turned to good account in a national service new army if it were trained without unnecessary "bull" and modernised with all the latest technical devices—including splendidly accoutred motor-cycles. At the moment—through lack of imagination and the absence of any organisation for group activity in music, dancing and singing, international travel and cultural contacts with other nations—this surplus energy is being run to waste in rowdyism, rioting, racing and many other exciting but brainless occupations such as playing death on the roads. We spend almost as much money on gambling as we do on education,[1] which suggests that our society, although it is tolerant, liberal and decent by comparison with many others, has very little serious purpose.

It is surely time that we got one. It should not be so difficult. We could dedicate ourselves to founding an advanced industrial society where decent adult human relationships take the place of the present haggling over the hire of labour as a mere commodity in the industrial process. We could devote ourselves to the scientific study of human behaviour and try to reach an integration of the freely developing individual personality with the group functioning of an industrial state combining public and private enterprise. This would be solving our own particular British problem but even so it would be a contribution to the whole western world and perhaps a step towards the co-operation which must eventually come between West and East. It would be wonderful to play a part in world affairs greater than being a mere extension of Anglo-Saxon affluence where every one is crowing "We've never had it so good". That could be the cry of a dying civilisation.

[1] The Education votes for 1962-63 required £992·7 million—£884 million (local authorities) and £108·7 million (central government). The Churches' Council on Gambling estimated that £853 million was spent on betting of all sorts in 1962, horses £540 million, greyhounds £116 million, football pools £85½ million, football (fixed odds) £60 million, bingo £30 million, funfairs £7½ million. This, of course, is a gross turnover figure. The net cost to the public (after winnings) is probably around £200 million.

TWO

# THE WIDENING GULF

ALL SOCIETIES except the primitive are divided. The monolithic ones behind the Iron Curtain have the cracks plastered over, but underneath there is a deep division between the rulers and the ruled. In his early writings, from which he subsequently departed, Marx had recognised that replacement of private by collective ownership would not necessarily lessen the alienation of the working class.[1] Whenever work is imposed upon them from outside, that is, whenever work is not spontaneous, the working class, he said, would acquire a sense of alienation. This was certainly true of the British during the industrial revolution and since the turn of the present century the gulf between our minority ruling clique and the majority working mass has remained unbridged. Indeed, we have contrived since the war to sharpen the sense of alienation which the working class still feel and a clash of class interests has developed. In the last twelve years the harsh monetary policies which the Conservative ruling clique evolved to combat the apparent trend towards a wage-cost inflation brought the two sides of the nation into sharp confrontation. Often they found themselves bitterly opposed over a wage dispute, which stupid economic policies had brought to a head, and when that happened they were each inclined to behave foolishly and neurotically as though they were under the compulsive, subconscious drive of the class war. We are, in fact, still a split society exploited by two opposing interests each motivated solely by the acquisitive instinct. Such a split society tends to be a neurotic society. It is well known that over-developed acquisitive instincts are a form of neurosis masking a sense of insecurity.

It is significant that the improved material well-being of the masses—the good eating and living which most working men now enjoy—has not changed their habits or made them feel less segregated. They still maintain their own standards of behaviour, their own way of life untouched by middle-class

[1] *Economic and Philosophical Manuscripts.* See Professor J. M. Cameron's review article "A Last Look at Marxism" in *Encounter*, October 1963.

conventionalities. It is a mistake to suppose that because some miners have bought their own shoot[1] the workers are acquiring the outlook and reactions of the upper class. On the contrary, they remain their own highly individual segregated selves. The frontier dividing the working class from the rest of society persists and only the very gifted few among the working mass, who have had the benefit of higher education and have been able to cross the language barrier, reach and merge with the managerial and governing class.

What is not generally appreciated is that the division in society between "them", the governing clique, and "us", the governed working mass, is likely to be widened and not narrowed by the national pursuit of growth to which we are now rightly committed. The British way of life does not tolerate a hectic rate of expansion but at any rate we all want to see the national product increasing at a faster rate than the population. We all endorsed Butler's famous declaration that we could double our standard of living in a generation. Faster growth has therefore become a major national objective for government, managements and unions alike. But as long as we have no idea how the extra wealth should be divided between workers and employers are we not bound to heighten the tension between them?

Some may argue that if the policy of faster growth is making social tension worse it should be dropped. This would no doubt please a large part of the population because no one can claim that we British are naturally a work-loving people like the Chinese or the Germans. Most of us prefer wasting time over the television set or going to the races or watching some form of ball game or just mucking about in the garden. Being a sane, easy-going, happy people we do not regard work as a complete end in itself, unless, which is rare, it offers craftsmanship in which we can take a pride. But there is little chance that a government will be elected in the near future which stands for a policy of anti-growth. "Vote for me and see Britain decline" is not a slogan which will ensure much success at the polls, although it is what many candidates have been standing for at general elections for a very long time. The policy of growth must therefore be accepted as politically

[1] Fifteen miners, all regulars of the Pheasant Inn, Barnsley, Yorkshire, have leased 600 acres of moor and forest for week-end shooting parties (item in *Daily Mail*, 1961).

inevitable, if socially not very popular, and the more it is pressed the more argument there is going to be about the way in which the extra cake is cut.

Economically a national policy of growth is, of course, essential. We have a large population of over fifty-four million on a small island lacking all useful materials except coal and in order to maintain our high standard of living we have to use our native skills in making goods for export to pay for our essential imports of food and industrial materials. The deficiency between exports and imports—the trade gap—is paid for by various services to foreigners and by drawing dividends from our overseas investments. If we do not pursue a national policy of expansion, and if output per man rises more slowly in this country than in others, then, unless our real wages are also lagging behind, our prices will rise relative to others and our competitive position will be worsened.[1] That briefly is the economic case for a national policy of sustained economic growth. If we did not have to pay our way abroad we could idle to our hearts' content.

Growth must therefore be pursued and when it is further advanced we can begin to argue about the uses to which it is put—whether we should introduce colour television or educational television, whether we should have more private gadgetry or more public housing, whether we should have more bowling alleys or better mental health. As F. T. Blackaby[2] told the meeting of the British Association in 1962: "The pursuit of growth is materialistic only in the sense that all economics is materialistic—it is concerned with goods and services produced for sale. Growth does not have to imply an increase only in the production of the hated cars and television sets; it can just as well be an increase in the output of probation officers and psychiatric social workers if we want it that way." We will certainly need it that way if we join in the neurotic American race for material status symbols.

Heaven knows that we have an immense amount of social investment to do. We talk glibly of our affluent society but we are at a very early stage of affluence. It has been calculated[2]

[1] See J. R. Sargent in Fabian Tract 343: "*Out of Stagnation*", 1963.

[2] By F. T. Blackaby, editor of the *Economic Review* of the National Institute of Economic and Social Research. See his paper on "The Recent Performance of the British Economy" read at the meeting of the British Association for the Advancement of Science, August 1962.

that if our gross national product had grown since 1955 as fast as that of the slowest-growing member of the European Economic Community, which is Holland, we should have had £2,500 million more resources at our disposal in the year 1961 when Selwyn Lloyd imposed his pay pause. Translate this vast sum into terms of social investment—houses, hospitals, clinics, schools and concert halls, not to mention motor-ways and national parks—and you will realise how the lack of adequate economic growth has prevented the nation from offering its citizens a fuller, healthier and more cultural life. We are now madly rushing ahead with motor-cars and television before we have even cleared the slums or stamped out poverty.[1] In other words we are building the wrong sort of society because we lack a sense of national unity and purpose.

There have been plenty of critics to sneer at the grossly materialistic society which seems to be developing—call it "the affluent society" or "the acquisitive society" or "the stagnant society" or what you will[2]—but there is little agreement upon the sort of society we ought to try to create. The prevailing emphasis lies heavily on expansion and the accumulation of wealth but no one seems to be conscious of the increasing mal-distribution of private wealth which is one of the bizarre effects of a public policy of growth without social direction. As both political parties are applying a growth policy in a still free, if mixed, economy it is pretty certain what the result will be—the better-educated rich will get richer far more quickly than the less-educated poor will get less poor. The same trend is to be found in international affairs: the rich highly-developed nations are getting richer far more quickly than the poor under-developed nations are getting less poor. The gulf between rich and poor is becoming wider throughout the world.

To increase the inequalities of wealth in our present state

[1] Peter Townsend, after examining the Ministry of Labour data collected in the family expenditure survey of 1953-54, found that nearly 3% of the population lived below the 1960 basis of National Assistance rates plus rent and another 8½% less than 40% above these rates. They comprised about six million people. Another one million could be added for persons dependent on National Assistance but living in households more than 40% above these rates (*New Statesman*, 20th April 1962).

[2] *The Affluent Society* by Professor J. K. Galbraith, Hamish Hamilton, 1958; "The Acquisitive Society" from *Income Distribution and Social Change—a study in criticism* by Professor R. Titmuss, Allen and Unwin, 1962 and *The Stagnant Society—a warning* by Michael Shanks, Penguin Books, 1962.

of social tension is surely asking for trouble. Even the mild George Woodcock was so incensed when Selwyn Lloyd arbitrarily imposed his pay pause in 1961 that he advised his fellow trade unionists to resist, if necessary, by force. And Frank Cousins was able to say without contradiction at the Trades Union Congress in September 1963, that labour would never agree to a wage restraint policy under a Conservative Government. Clearly there are still two nations, not one, and the most urgent task awaiting statesmanship today is to bring them together.

At the moment the only meeting ground the two "nations" have got is the not very solid N.E.D.C. (National Economic Development Council) on which the trade unions and the employers are represented at the highest level under the chairmanship of the Chancellor of the Exchequer. When the Labour party regains power this Council will no doubt be re-shaped in the national scheme for reconstruction but as I write it is a monument to the growing split in our society. It proclaims with every report that no agreement is possible on a national incomes policy between employers and employees. I will explain the reason why in what follows—but what growth, what riches we could all have if we were to become a united nation a little less concerned with betting, a little more interested in work, a little more serious in purpose!

And a little more intelligent! In a country where devotion to sport, fair play and being kind to animals assume the status of a national religion it needed a continuum of incredible stupidity on the part of the ruling clique to keep the working class alienated. By "clique" I mean the governing bodies in the City, in Parliament, in Whitehall and in big business outside and for reasons which will be given I include within this Establishment some leaders of the Parliamentary Labour party. By "alienate" I mean exactly what the dictionary says. The tough economic measures which the Establishment has persistently taken to protect the exchange value of the £ have not merely caused the working classes to "withdraw their affection", but have made them indifferent to—and on occasions blindly averse to—the interests of the nation as a whole. In short, financial and economic mismanagement has been responsible for maintaining the dangerous division in our society.

This tragedy has been enacted within the lifetime of the

generation into which I was born. I have therefore been able to follow it closely and I have noted five stages which in 1961 led to the most dangerous clash with the working class seen since the general strike in 1926. As I am dealing in this sociological-economic analysis always with the state of the public mind I have distinguished these five stages by psychiatric terms as follows: Stress (the 1920s), Depression (the 1930s), Sublimaation (the war years), Frustration and Disillusionment (the Labour régime, 1945-51) and Pathological Cynicism (the Tory régime, 1951-64). By the time the fifth stage was reached our whole society had become neurotic. Aldous Huxley once defined a neurotic individual as a person "who responds to the challenges of the present in terms of the obsessively remembered past". This describes exactly the state of mind of both the working class and the ruling clique when they found themselves starkly opposed during Selwyn Lloyd's heavy and clumsy handling of the incomes policy. It is fortunate that he was sacked and replaced by a more balanced Chancellor, Reginald Maudling, who mollified Labour by presenting in 1963 a budget they could not fault either in social justice or in expansionist fervour. But let me start with the 1920s.

# PART II

# THE HISTORICAL ANALYSIS

THREE

# STRESS IN THE 'TWENTIES

I FIRST BECAME AWARE that the ruling clique was losing its grasp of economic affairs when I began to write financial articles on the invitation of Maynard Keynes and Hubert Henderson[1] nearly forty years ago. Although I had gone up to Oxford on a history scholarship I met Keynes through an undergraduate friend who was up at King's College, Cambridge. In 1922 Keynes was editing the famous supplements of the *Manchester Guardian* on "Reconstruction in Europe" and I had contributed an occasional article on international oil on which I had just written a book.[2] In 1923 Keynes took the lead of a group of fellow Liberals in buying control of the *Nation and Athenaeum*. Henderson, a distinguished Cambridge economist, became the editor and he and Keynes asked me to write the financial page. This work, which continued when the *Nation* merged with the *New Statesman*, brought me up against the incredibly cruel economic régime which the government was imposing on the working class in preparation for the return to gold. That a minority ruling clique should exacerbate the workers within a few years of the bloody Russian Revolution, that it should provoke them—almost beyond endurance—by forcing down their wages, throwing them out of work and offering them semi-starvation on a miserable dole, made me think that they had all taken leave of their senses. At first I was afraid that I was catching some of the intellectual arrogance from which Keynes at that time suffered, but Henderson, who had a gentle and sympathetic nature, convinced me that Keynes's ferocious criticism of official stupidity was correct and just. The ruling clique had, in fact, sunk into mental and moral decay. It had not only stopped using its brains; it had become insensitive to suffering.

A psychiatrist could probably give a simple explanation of this decline and rot. The First World War had been a great shock to the governing class—they had come near to losing

[1] Later Sir Hubert Henderson, Warden elect of All Souls before his death in 1952.

[2] *The Oil Trusts and Anglo-American Relations*, Macmillan, 1923.

the war in 1917—and it had left them mentally and physically exhausted. The flower of a brilliant generation had perished and the survivors were bewildered. Just when their perceptions had become dulled they were called upon to deal with complicated social, economic and political problems of which they had had no previous experience. A sharp post-war boom and slump, increasing unemployment, growing industrial unrest, economic chaos in Europe, a currency collapse in Germany, communism becoming more militant and threatening and, finally, fascism raising its ugly head in Italy and later in Germany—all these frightening events seemed to them beyond the scope of gentlemen whose thinking is usually done for them by the higher Civil Service. As a result they began to lose their nerve as well as their senses.

The trouble was that they could not adjust their thinking to the changed position of the nation in world affairs. They had seen Great Britain shrink from world supremacy in sea power to a second-class status in air power and industrial power and they could not bear to think of it. They clung desperately to the memory of the great and glorious past, the twin symbols of which had been the Crown and the £ sterling. At the time the Crown was slowly regaining popularity but the £ sterling had lost its glitter; it had been divorced from gold.[1] It seemed obvious to them that at all costs the £ must be put back on to gold at its old parity.

Keynes had criticised and attacked the gold standard long before he condemned the return to gold at the old parity in 1925. He disliked the gold standard because it entailed as part of its regular and normal operation the creation from time to time of surplus capacity and massive unemployment. A system which required the imposition of human idleness and suffering—as a means of checking an inflation—was, he felt, both senseless and inhuman. Any rational being educated in the humanist tradition would have agreed with him. But not the British Establishment. These pompous defenders of the *status quo* were determined to return to gold at the old rate. Keynes and Henderson warned them that to do so would be to over-value the £ by about 10%—it was then quoted at 10% discount on the gold dollar—and that this would depress the export trades, create worse unemployment and force down wages. Their

[1] When the dollar exchange had been unpegged after the war an Act was passed in 1920 prohibiting the export of gold except on licence.

warnings were disregarded. The Treasury persuaded the Ministers that the discrepancy between American and British prices was only 2½% in favour of America. The Ministers declared that the return to gold would bring a more competitive spirit into industry and enhance the national prestige. They wanted the £ "to look the dollar in the eye". They pointed to the disaster which had befallen the German mark which Schacht had finally stabilised by issuing one new rentenmark for one million-million old marks. The idea that such a catastrophe could happen in Britain was, of course, ludicrous,[1] but for them the restoration of the gold £ was a desirable end in itself and when they began thinking in "hard" money terms they ceased to think in compassionate human terms. Keynes prophesied industrial unrest. The working class, he said, would be subjected to a cut in money wages without any guarantee that there would be a fall in the cost of living. "They are bound to resist so long as they can and it must be war until those who are economically weaker are beaten to the ground."[2] In spite of his denunciations the £ was put back on to gold at its old parity in the budget speech of 28th April 1925.[3]

The Chancellor of the Exchequer at the time was Winston Churchill, who knew so little about economics that he told the House of Commons that the return to gold was no more responsible for the distress in the coal industry than the Gulf Stream. Keynes had contemptuously referred to ministerial statements of this kind as "feather-brained" in his devastating pamphlet called *The Economic Consequences of Mr. Churchill*. Again he warned the Government that industrial unrest would follow. The working classes could not be expected, he said, to understand what is happening better than Cabinet Ministers who, he implied, were just a bunch of ignorami.

What in fact these ignorami had done was to confuse ends and means. The preservation of a particular exchange rate in terms of gold is not an end in itself—not even as a matter of prestige. The exchange rate for the £ sterling is only a means to

[1] Germany had been a defeated nation forced to pay heavy reparations in cash and kind. The appalling shortage of goods had led to rocketing prices and despair and when the French marched into the Rhineland in January 1923 the mark began its catastrophic descent.

[2] "The Economic Consequences of Mr. Churchill" republished in *Essays in Persuasion* by J. M. Keynes, Macmillan, 1931.

[3] The 1920 gold suspension Act expired in 1925 and by allowing it to lapse the Government put the £ back on gold automatically.

an end—the end being a healthy and expanding economy in which supplies can be imported at reasonable prices and goods can be produced and exported at competitive prices and in sufficient volume to meet the deficit on the visible trade account. If the particular rate of exchange is not bringing about that desirable result, then soon or later it will have to be changed, as indeed it has been—not infrequently. No one can now say that there is anything sacrosanct about the sterling exchange when the £ has been devalued in 1914, upvalued in 1925, devalued in 1931, allowed to float from 1931 to 1939, again devalued in 1939 and finally slashed in value (by 30%) in 1949. To go back deliberately to a higher rate of exchange in 1925, which was bound to damage the export trade and induce a slump, was a *folie de grandeur*.

It was clear that the ruling clique in 1925 had a concept of Britain entirely divorced from the interests of the working population. It desired to see the overseas investments of the nation built up and the international banking business of the City flourish regardless of the state of unemployment at home. The finance houses in the City were not at that time interested in domestic industry: they knew far more about the commercial needs of South America or the capital requirements of South Africa with its gold mines than about Lancashire, Yorkshire, Tyneside or the Clyde. When they staged a new issue boom in the late 'twenties it was primarily a company promoter's affair—dishing out huge cash profits to the vendors of some speculative business or to the inventors of some new gadget for the affluent consumer. Week after week Keynes, Henderson and I would expose the inefficiencies, the wastefulness, the immoralities of the prevailing financial system in our weekly press but the Government went on allowing money to be pumped into the financial machine without seeing that it came out in the form of useful productive industrial investment which could put the unemployed millions into work. The finance—capitalism of the 1920s and 1930s may have provided thick bread and butter for the City, but it dropped precious few crumbs for the working class.

The arch-priest of the financial Establishment in 1925 was Montagu Norman, Governor of the Bank of England. He was typical of the hide-bound attitude to economic affairs which these blind defenders of the ancient past adopted. O. T. Falk, the brilliant financier friend of Keynes, who had been an unofficial adviser of Montagu Norman up to this point, told me that when he opposed the restoration of the old gold parity of the £ and had advocated devaluation, the Governor sent for him and solemnly declared in his parlour: "I don't know what you mean by devaluation: I have heard of default." The mystique of the £, like the mystique of the Crown, was always part of the blind faith of the British Establishment.

That a ruling minority clique could subject the mass working population deliberately to the scourge of unemployment for the sake of a gold £ and the prosperity of the City of London seemed to me incredible at the time. To the simple uneducated working man a job is his life. Jobless he is left without respect in his own home. Pitied he loses respect for himself. He is not long out of work before a lowering of his ego sets in and when semi-starvation is added his body rots as quickly as his soul. I had seen it with my own eyes because at that time I used to talk to miners' clubs in public house parlours. The deliberate degradation and brutalisation of working men, which the policy of deflation entailed in 1925, were not only a provocation of the working class but a crime against humanity. At that time there was no question of a choice between inflation and deflation. There had been no threat of inflation since the collapse of the speculative boom in 1920. Deflation may have been justified in 1920 but certainly not in 1925. When deflation is carried to the point of inflicting massive unemployment and bringing about a redistribution of real income in favour of the rentier class it must always be a social crime.[1] Bankers even today have not grasped this elementary point.

Exactly as Keynes and Henderson had warned, unemployment grew worse after the return to gold. By December 1926, it had risen by nearly 25% to 1,432,000. The old staple industries, coal, iron and steel, shipbuilding, cotton textiles, which had over-expanded in the short post-war boom, were already in decline. The "distressed areas" were emerging. What the country was needing was not a severe deflation

[1] Keynes wrote in 1932 in *A Tract on Monetary Reform*: "Deflation envolves a transference of wealth from the rest of the community to the rentier class and to all holders of titles to money, just as inflation envolves the opposite. In particular it envolves a transference from all borrowers, that is, from traders, manufacturers and farmers to lenders—from the active to the inactive."

forcing wages to be cut but the rationalisation of industry and the modernisation of industrial plants. There were far too many small uneconomic units in all the staple industries. The techniques used in the backward parts of the coal industry were much behind the advanced techniques used in other countries. The Liberal industrial inquiry (published in 1928 as "Britain's Industrial Future") was later on to find and expose an obstinate prejudice among the industrial leaders against all forms of rationalisation. The employers simply preferred wage cuts to modernisation.

Meanwhile, the coalowners persisted in their demands for a substantial cut in miners' wages. The Samuel Commission, reporting in March 1926, recommended that a cut should be made, not by as much as the owners had demanded but by enough to bring real wages down to below the pre-1914 level. Driven to desperation, the miners struck and with the left-wing leaders then in temporary control of the trade unions the general strike followed on 5th May. In six days it had collapsed. The trade union leaders, disavowing any revolutionary intentions, had realised the dangerous revolutionary possibilities and had hastened to bring the strike to an end. J. H. Thomas said in the House of Commons: "I have never disguised the fact that in a challenge to the constitution God help us unless the constitution won." Ellen Wilkinson reported that a miner had said to her: "If the British constitution makes a man work underground for less than £2 a week, it's about time that constitution was challenged." But there was no leadership at the top to give direction to the rank and file.

The ignominious collapse of the general strike marked a further stage in the alienation of the British working class. It sowed the first seeds of suspicion among the workers that they could not rely on their own parliamentary spokesmen. This seed was to grow twenty-one years later, when Cripps tried to apply his austerity to current wage claims, into an actual trade union discontent with a Labour administration.

Incidentally it was the general strike which brought the late Hugh Gaitskell into the Labour movement. The social injustices which he had seen inflicted in the name of a false economic law had made an ardent social reformer out of this young intellectual economist. Social reform moved the hearts of so many more who were not intellectuals that within three years the Labour Party was returned at a general election as the largest party in the State. It was significant that in this 1929 election, when Labour won 287 seats, the Conservatives 260 and the Liberals 59, the Communists lost every one of the twenty-five seats they had contested. This marked the turning-away of the Labour movement from direct industrial action to parliamentary democracy. The workers were giving another chance, as it were, to their parliamentary spokesmen to prove that they could be relied upon and would not betray the workers' cause. It was unfortunate that at this critical hour their leaders in Parliament turned out to be traitors to the Labour cause—the vacillating MacDonald, the compromising Thomas and the narrow-minded Snowden. It was this terrible trio that had to deal with the onslaught of the great depression and the exchange crisis of 1931.

FOUR

# DEPRESSION IN THE 'THIRTIES

A WONDERFUL OPPORTUNITY was presented to the Parliamentary Labour party in the 1930s to win the confidence of the workers. The Conservative Government had failed to do anything but create social discontent. For the first time in its history Labour was the largest party in the State and had the good will of the nation. Here was a chance to prove that it could apply some of the Keynesian theories to protect the British working man against the tidal wave of the deepening world depression. Hopes ran high when Snowden, as Chancellor of the Exchequer, appointed a Committee of Inquiry into Finance and Industry with lawyer Lord Macmillan in the chair and with Keynes, McKenna, Brand, Ernest Bevin and Professor Gregory as members. Finally, when an Economic Advisory Council was created in January 1930, with Hubert Henderson as its secretary and with Keynes among its members, there was a widespread feeling that at long last some useful official action was being taken which might help to solve the increasingly alarming problem of unemployment.

At the famous confrontation with Montagu Norman during the meetings of the Macmillan Committee, Keynes, aided and abetted by Ernest Bevin, had actually forced an admission from the Governor of the Bank that the main purpose of raising Bank rate was to create unemployment.[1] An evil exposed is usually half-destroyed. To expose the evil social consequences of the orthodox banking policy was, we Keynesians hoped, sufficient to get that policy eliminated or radically changed. But we were all too childishly optimistic. We had not yet realised how dangerous it was to believe in rational man. The deeply ingrained stupidity of the Establishment was not to be dislodged by reason but by suffering. MacDonald and Snowden learned nothing and took nothing from Keynes or Henderson. They pursued the same foolish type of economic

[1] In the minutes of evidence at the Macmillan Committee the following occurs: *Keynes*: "So it is of the essence of the case that the Bank rate should have an important effect: that when it is raised it should have an effect in the direction of unemployment. That is what you want. Am I right?

*Norman:* "Yes, I should think it was."

policy as their predecessors. Their vision was just as limited: their industrial programme just as unimaginative and their political actions just as restricted by financial orthodoxy. The pity of it was that the suffering they inflicted had to be borne—before the policies were changed—by innocent working people. The only Labour leader at this time who learned something from Keynes was Ernest Bevin who, after that debate with Norman at the Macmillan Committee, never lost his hatred of the gold standard. Alas, when he came to power later on he was denied the chance to put his liberal economic ideas into practice: he was switched from the Treasury to the Foreign Office by his short-sighted party leader.

In October 1929 the great Wall Street crash had startled the financial world—wiping $16,000 million off the value of equity shares in a single day—and businessmen everywhere were losing their nerve, abandoning their spending plans and cutting down their commitments. When the MacDonald administration took office the army of unemployed numbered 1,164,000 and by January 1930 it had risen to 1,520,000. There was no seasonal improvement in the spring. In April 2,070,000 were workless, in July 2,319,000 and in October 2,500,000. The alarming American collapse helped to intensify and widen the world trade depression. In Germany nearly 4,500,000 men were out of work. British exports, which had been £848 million in 1929, fell to £666 million in 1930 and eventually to £461 million in 1931. Chancellor Snowden, worrying himself sick about the £, could only think of balancing the budget and cutting incomes. He told the House of Commons: "An expenditure which may be easy and tolerable in prosperous times becomes intolerable in a time of grave industrial depression." This one sentence revealed how deeply the banking orthodoxy had taken possession of him. The pathetic J. H. Thomas, Lord Privy Seal, had been put in charge of employment and was given three ministerial assistants, one of whom was Oswald Mosley. It was ironic that Mosley was the only minister to resign—in May 1930—in protest against Snowden's deflationary policies. His manifesto was signed by seventeen leftish members of Parliament, including Aneurin Bevan and John Strachey.

In February 1931, Snowden, more worried than ever because foreign bankers were beginning to lose confidence in the £, appointed Sir George May, secretary of the Prudential, to lead a committee to advise on cuts in the pay of Government servants (including the Services) and in the dole. Snowden uttered all the well-known clichés of the bankers. "Drastic and disagreeable measures", he said, "will have to be taken if the Budget equilibrium is to be maintained and if industrial progress is to be made." Of course the drastic and disagreeable meaures fell most heavily on the workers and the unemployed. By May the unemployed army had risen to 2,600,000, by June to 2,707,000 and by July to 2,800,000. The £ came under heavy selling pressure and the Bank began to lose gold. The strain was too much for Montagu Norman. At the beginning of August he suffered a breakdown and was shipped off to Canada for a complete rest.

In August the May Report was published—the two Labour leaders dissenting. It shocked Keynes who described it as "the most foolish document I have ever had the misfortune to read". It also shocked the public with its drastic slashing of the salaries of police, teachers and the armed services, a 10% cut in the dole and higher contributions to the national insurance scheme. A flight from the £ immediately followed. The foreign bankers—American and French—made it clear that no further loans would be granted to save the £ unless the Government balanced its budget on the lines recommended in the May Report. This "bankers' ramp" caused a Cabinet split and MacDonald went off to the King to betray his colleagues and to accept the King's nomination to head a National Government with his faithful servants Thomas and Snowden (still Chancellor) and with Baldwin as Lord President of the Council.

The new Government immediately complied with the May Report and imposed the hated means test for national insurance. But the £ was not saved. The cut in Service pay produced a mutiny in the fleet at Invergordon. Sterling was heavily sold and the Bank began to lose gold at the rate of £2½ million a day. So the old gold £ could not be saved: the May Report had killed it. On 21st September it was divorced from gold—as Keynes had in fact recommended. It fell from $4.86 to $3.23—to the great relief and stimulus of the export trade. Two days later Montagu Norman returned to London—as free from stress as sterling—and was no doubt pleased to see the £ settle down before the end of the year at around $3.40. Thereafter exchange rate flexibility took the financial strain.[1]

[1] The exchange rate for dollars averaged 3.50 in 1932, 4.22 in 1933 (when the dollar was devalued), 5.04 in 1934, 4.97 in 1936, 4.94 in 1937, 4.89 in 1938. It was lowered to 4.46 in 1939 and pegged at 4.03 during the Second World War.

The operations of the Exchange Equalisation Fund protected and insulated the domestic economy and made possible the return to lower rates for money and to better economic growth.

Coming so soon after the savage deflation of 1925-26, this new attack on the standard of living of the working class caused bitter resentment. The rank and file could never again have the same feeling towards their parliamentary leaders. True, the loyal Arthur Henderson was leading the opposition to MacDonald and was supported by Attlee, Dalton, Morrison and the rest, but how could the workers ever again be sure that their Parliament men would not let them down when the next financial crisis came? The fact that MacDonald, Thomas and Snowden had run panic-stricken to the financial Establishment when they got into trouble suggested to the man in the street that working-class politicians were incapable of coping with complicated matters of finance. This may explain why a third or more of the working class still refuse to vote Labour at general elections.

The harsh household means test pushed the estrangement of the working class a step further. Angry demonstrations, hunger marches, riots and arrests followed one another in 1932.[1] "For the first time within memory", wrote G. K. Chesterton, "the Government and the nation have set out on a definite deliberate campaign to make the poor poorer." He was not exaggerating. When the meagre national insurance benefit had been exhausted, a man and his family had to prove need before he could obtain national assistance. Here are two examples of inhumanity from the many cases quoted by the T.U.C. in a protest they made to the Government. On Tyneside there was an out-of-work man with an invalid wife and ten children, seven of them of school age. One girl of sixteen was earning eight shillings a week, one boy of fourteen was unemployed and another in the army was sending home 5*s*. 3*d*. This man had his benefit reduced from 37*s*. 9*d*. to 21*s*. 9*d*. Another unemployed worker in Wigan had his benefit cut from 23*s*. 3*d*. to 10*s*. a week because he had two sons earning between them 31*s*. a week.

In the two years to October 1933, according to a Ministry of Labour report, the economies effected by the cut in the dole and the means test amounted to only about £27 million each —£54 million "wrung from the most poverty-stricken section of the community", as the Communist march leader, Wal

[1] See *Britain Between the Wars, 1918-1940* by C. L. Mowat, Methuen, 1955.

Hannington, wrote in his book on the distressed areas.[1] The memory of these savage economies exacted for the sake of the exchange rate of the £ left behind a bitterness in the working class which has remained to this day. In my home country in north-west Berkshire elderly farm workers still speak of the days when they took home only 30*s*. a week if they were lucky enough to be employed. A plumber I know was then working at 1*s*. 6*d*. an hour in the building industry. The miners had to work a seven or eight-hour shift, cutting coal at 6*d*. a ton, in order to take home not much over 40*s*. a week. Allowing for all the difference in the purchasing power of the £ it was a scandalously low wage.

It is something to the credit of Neville Chamberlain, who took over the chancellorship from Snowden in MacDonald's second National Government (November 1931, to June 1935) that he made use of the divorce from gold by cheapening money, pulling down the rate of interest to help the finance of trade and industrial investment. By the middle of 1932 the Bank rate had fallen to 2% (it had been put up to 6% in September 1931) and the great *tranche* of War Loan (nearly £2,000 million) had been converted from a 5% to a 3½% coupon. But Chamberlain failed to do as much with cheap money as Keynes would have done in the actual creation of employment. A housing drive was started but little else. No one (not even Keynes) had yet thought of building half a dozen new towns or reconstructing some of the out-of-date industrial "infrastructure" of the country. Expenditure on roads, for example, which was only £19 million in 1931 and 1932, fell to £8 million by 1936. Some relief came to the working class in 1934 by the restoration of the cuts in the dole but more to the rich by the cut in income tax from 5*s*. to 4*s*. 6*d*. The old salary scales in the public services were restored by 1935. At this point Chamberlain made his only memorable remark: "We have left Bleak House and might now begin *Great Expectations*." It was not a joke appreciated by the working class, for the hated means test remained.

When Baldwin became premier in place of MacDonald in June 1935, a bigger effort was made to reduce unemployment in the "distressed areas". A Special Areas Act was passed and Special Commissioners were appointed—Sir Malcolm Stuart for England and Wales and Sir Arthur Rose for Scotland—to propose schemes for greater employment in these areas. Both

[1] *The Problem of the Distressed Areas* by Wal Hannington, published as a paper-back by the Left Book Club, Gollancz, 1937.

knights soon retired from the field in despair. They had no power to secure finance for the schemes they proposed and they invariably found that they were blocked by the vested interests on the spot. For example, Sir Malcolm proposed a new steel works at Jarrow but the Iron and Steel Federation opposed it because it would take profits away from existing steel companies. In spite of the protest marches of workers from Jarrow to Westminster in October 1936, the Government did nothing. Sir Malcolm said before his resignation: "To bring the unemployment of the Special Areas down to even 25% (the mean between their average figure of unemployment and that of England and Wales) would be a very considerable achievement but frankly I do not see any prospect of any effective reduction under existing conditions."

The political dice seemed to be loaded against the working class. Capitalism had produced an appalling economic and social mess and the National Government was incapable of rescuing the wretched working men and women who were caught up in the tragedy. It was a tragedy which moved prominent Conservatives and Liberals as well as Labour people. In 1935 Macmillans published a book called *The Next Five Years*, by authors of different politics and parties, as an essay in political agreement. It was signed, among others, by Harold Macmillan. It advocated economic planning and growth and the re-organisation of industry and although it rejected nationalisation of the joint stock banks it recommended turning the banks into public utilities with a limitation of their profits. The National Government, however, would have no radicalism. It would have none of the Keynesian theories of spending its way out of depression. Chamberlain, who became Prime Minister in May 1937, was not a man to have unbalanced budgets. It was not until rearmament against the growing Nazi menace caused the Government to spend enough money on shipbuilding and the armed forces to relieve unemployment that life and wages became more reasonable for the working man. But the sufferings of the great depression will never be forgotten in the Labour movement. It was a traumatic experience which has left its scar on the drawn faces of the older generation of workers. It was lucky that we escaped a bloody, violent revolution. Perhaps, after all, the Marxist Clause 4 of the Labour Party constitution had its uses as a safety-valve. It tricked the patient working masses into thinking that the Parliamentary Labour party were on their side.

FIVE

# SUBLIMATION IN THE WAR YEARS

DURING THE WAR years there was a sublimation of the social conflict. Every class put the safety of the nation above its own self-interest. But Labour did not transfer its aspirations to the national war drive until its leaders had joined the Coalition Government under Churchill. The trade unions were then prepared to pull together with the Government in the national struggle for survival. For the time being the workers had confidence in their parliamentary spokesmen—an event which had not been seen since 1918.

It was an accepted principle of the coalition that on the civil front the organisations of capital and labour shared the exercise of economic power while at the Ministry of Labour ruled the great trade unionist, Ernest Bevin. The coalition worked so smoothly and efficiently that I began to be afraid that after the war these powerful organisations of capital and labour would carry their co-operation a step too far and found the managerial State in which the consumer would be unmercifully exploited. Encouraged by Bernard Shaw, who assured me on one of his post-cards that "State-aided capitalism is Fascism", I wrote a book called *Vested Interests or Common Pool?* in which the danger of the corporate state was rudely exposed.[1] But the danger happily passed away when the Parliamentary Labour party remained true to its first principles and refused to join the Churchill "caretaker" government after the war.

The war stirred up the social conscience of the nation. Every Minister of State from Churchill downwards felt that the workers were entitled, when peace came, to full employment and social security. Coming not long after Dunkirk—while the Dunkirk spirit ruled—a succession of White Papers poured out from the departments on such matters as improved national insurance, supplementary pensions, family allowances, education and health, free milk and subsidised meals at school, in fact, the complete package of the modern Welfare State. The nation had decided once and for all to make an end of the

[1] Published by Victor Gollancz, 1943.

hardships and cruelties of *laissez faire* capitalism and so complete the work which Lloyd George had begun in the great Liberal administration before the First World War.

The height of this social idealism was expressed in the famous White Paper of May 1944 on Employment Policy (Cmnd. 6527). This committed all post-war governments to the practice of the Keynesian theory of full employment and growth which had been evolved during the great depression. It was the joint effort of the Treasury (John Anderson), the Ministry of Reconstruction (Woolton) and the Board of Trade (Dalton), who had all been instructed to study the problems of post-war reconstruction. The draughtsmen were the outside economists temporarily employed in the Treasury. Dalton had been writing a policy paper for the Labour National Executive on "Full Employment and Financial Policy" in April 1944, in which he had fought for iron and steel to be included in the list of industries which his party had determined to nationalise after the war.[1] He was delighted that he was able to get his memorandum out in print before the Treasury White Paper. His main concern, his constituency being in a depressed north-east region, was to solve the special problem of local unemployment by directing companies and industries to the so-called "distressed areas".

Now the White Paper ranged over the whole economy and expressed the pure Keynesian doctrine that full employment could only be secured nationally by "a policy for maintaining total internal expenditure". Of course the authors were well aware that there would be no problem of general unemployment in the years immediately after the war. That would be a period of shortage. "It is likely to be some time", they said, "before the need arises to put into operation the long-term policy for averting mass unemployment." The fascinating part of this far-seeing war-time Paper was that it committed the Conservative Party as well as Labour to a policy of full employment and expansion. In other words a "growth" Welfare State had become the objective of the two great political parties in Great Britain.

The Keynesian theories were clearly expressed in the foreword which ran as follows:

[1] If Dalton, the north-east coast champion, had not cast covetous eyes on iron and steel, it might never have been included in Labour's nationalisation list.

> The Government accept as one of their primary aims and responsibilities the maintenance of a high and stable level of employment after the war. . . . A country will not suffer from mass unemployment so long as the total demand for its goods and services is maintained at a high level.

The White Paper laid down three general conditions for "a high and stable level of employment":

para 39:
- (i) total expenditure on goods and services must be prevented from falling to a level where general unemployment appears;
- (ii) the level of prices and wages must be kept reasonably stable;
- (iii) there must be sufficient mobility of workers between occupations and localities.

The authors insisted that the Government must be ready to check and reverse any decline in consumer spending which might follow on a temporary drop in private investment or in exports but they showed that they were well aware of the inflationary risk of this spending policy because in paragraphs 49, 50, 51 and 52 they wrote:

> If we are to operate with success a policy for maintaining a high and stable level of employment it will be essential that employers and workers should exercise moderation in wages matters. This does not mean that every wage rate must remain fixed at a particular level. . . . The principle of stability does mean, however, that increases in the general level of wage rates must be related to increased productivity due to increased efficiency and effort. . . . An undue increase in prices due to causes other than increased wages might similarly frustrate action taken by the Government for maintaining employment. If, for example, the manufacturers in a particular industry were in a ring for the purpose of raising prices, additional money made available by Government action for the purpose of maintaining employment might simply be absorbed in increased profit margins and no increase in employment would result. Stability of wages and stability of prices are inextricably connected.

Thus the Labour Party as well as the Conservative was committed after the war not only to the attempt to iron out cyclical depressions in the Keynesian style by stepping up public expenditure in periods of sub-normal trade but to what is now known as a "wages policy"—the restriction of the rate of wage advances to the rate of increase in national productivity. Not only that: it was committed to action against restrictive practices in labour as well as in management. Paragraph 54 of the White Paper ran:

> Workers must examine their trade practices and customs to ensure that they do not constitute a serious impediment to an expansionist economy and so defeat the object of a full employment programme.

The Labour Ministers showed no hesitation at all in agreeing to these clauses. It was significant that the only opposition to the White Paper came from Aneurin Bevan. He saw that Keynesian theories could save capitalism from collapse and he just did not want to save or even reform the capitalist system. He wanted a socialist Britain after the war. He described the pledge "to sustain a high and stable level of employment" as a bare-faced attempt to side-step nationalisation and socialism. "These White Papers", he said, "are the blueprints of the coalition programme at the next general election. White Paper carrots! The donkey should watch out![1] He had the insight to see that the Labour party might be trapped into anti-socialist attitudes.

Ernest Bevin saw the White Paper differently. He welcomed it as the acceptance by all parties of the expansionist policy which he and Keynes had tried to urge on the Government in the nineteen-thirties at the Macmillan Committee. Dalton saw it as a wonderful opportunity to help "the distressed areas". He represented one in Parliament. If only Bevin had had Dalton's job when the war ended he might have got the economy running on sensible lines, for there is no doubt that he understood the modern industrial system better than his colleagues.

There is a foolish notion that after the war the Labour Government tried to apply in their ignorance the expansionist

[1] From *Aneurin Bevan; a biography* by Michael Foot, MacGibbon and Kee, 1963. Later on Bevan agreed with a wages policy and said so in his book *In Place of Fear*, Heinemann, 1952.

Keynesian policies of the 1944 White Paper in a situation which was the reverse of the one for which the policies were designed. Nothing of the sort happened. Nationalisation and the problems of transition from a war to a peace economy occupied their minds. The White Paper had warned them of the shortages they would meet and the risks of an inflationary rise in prices. Keynes did not die until 1946 and although he was busy negotiating the American loan he had opportunity enough to add his words of caution and advice. Besides, the White Paper had insisted that to avoid trouble the post-war Government would have to aim at a more balanced distribution of industry and at a greater diversification of trades, that it would have to train and re-educate workers for jobs in the expanding sectors and provide them with cheap new houses to rent in order to improve their mobility. This industrial and human reconstruction was lost sight of in the muddle and chaos which the far-reaching nationalisation programme entailed. The planning of new industrial investment was never attempted. Of course we can criticise the White Paper for its somewhat naïve and elementary methods for maintaining total expenditure, which we would now have to revise in the light of our new economic experience, but there is no doubt that it was an outstanding advance in the application of welfare economics to a modern industrial state.

Before the war-time coalition broke up Dalton managed by superhuman efforts—threatening at one time to resign if Churchill did not agree—to get the principles of the White Paper translated into action in his Distribution of Industry Bill. This empowered the Board of Trade to build factories and houses in "development" areas, to acquire and prepare land for that purpose, to help local companies to raise new capital for factory building or extension and finally to make loans to non-profit-making trading estates. A vital clause was inserted to require industrialists to notify the Board of Trade of their intention to build factories. This enabled a Labour Government later on to direct industry into the areas of high unemployment. It was a remarkable feat on Dalton's part to get the Royal Assent to this Act on 15th June 1945, the day when Parliament was to be dissolved. This was his finest hour —his greatest contribution to the relief of working-class distress. Whether it was the right way to improve the growth of a lop-sided economy is another question.

SIX

# SOCIALISM IN 1945

I MUST FIRST EXPLAIN how the Labour party came to fight and win the 1945 election on a full-blooded socialist programme. As everyone knows, Labour has never been a revolutionary party. It was formed in 1900 out of the union of various labour and socialist societies for the express purpose of sending representatives to Westminster—not as a Trojan horse for the overthrow of that citadel of democracy, but as a practical means of getting legislation passed to improve the pay and working conditions of the working class. That is why the great Liberal administration of 1906 won the enthusiastic support of the Labour movement for its radical programme of social reform. The Insurance Act of 1911 could be said to have laid the foundations of the modern Welfare State. Thanks to Labour support of the demagogic drive of Lloyd George the quick tempo of social change was sustained right up to 1914—and indeed until immediately after the war—in spite of the intense opposition of the Conservative forces entrenched in the House of Lords. But when the war ended there came social upheaval and discontent.

By this time the Labour movement had acquired a socialist ferment. The triple alliance which had been formed of miners, railwaymen and dockers in 1914, the shop stewards' movement, the Clyde Workers Committee, all were tending towards direct industrial action. The Russian Revolution of 1917 created immense excitement and there was even a mass meeting in Leeds to discuss the formation of workers' and soldiers' councils. In this electrifying atmosphere the Labour party acquired a new and socialistic constitution.[1] It was adopted at the conference in 1918 with the following national objectives:

1. To organise and maintain in Parliament and in the country a Political Labour Party.

[1] Under this constitution there had to be an executive committee of twenty-three members, of which thirteen represented the trade unions and five the local Labour parties. Four places were reserved for women. Thus, the trade union forces were given a perpetual majority of votes.

2. To co-operate with the General Council of the Trades Union Congress, or other kindred organisations, in joint political or other action in harmony with the Party Constitution and Standing Orders.
3. To give effect as far as may be practicable to the principles from time to time approved by the Party Conference.
4. To secure for the workers by hand or by brain the full fruits of their industry and the most suitable distribution thereof that may be possible upon the basis of the common ownership of the means of production and the best obtainable system of popular administration and control of each industry or service. (At the 1929 annual conference of the Labour party this clause was amended to read "the common ownership of the means of production distribution and exchange".)
5. Generally to promote the political, social and economic emancipation of the people and more particularly of those who depend directly upon their own exertions by hand or by brain for the means of life.

The party statement issued later under the title *Labour and the New Social Order* advocated the nationalisation of the land (by degrees), the railways, coal, electricity, gas, industrial life insurance, canals, harbours, docks and steamship lines and the entire manufacture and distribution of alcoholic drinks.

There was apparently no dispute between "right" and "left" over the Marxist-looking Clause 4. I am indebted to Mrs. Cole for correcting the wrong idea I once held that the "left" pressed this clause on the "right". In a letter to *The Spectator* of 22nd February 1963, she made it clear that it was the other way about: "If anything, Henderson was *le plus royaliste*. Beatrice Webb's diary of September 1919 records him as demanding that Webb should produce a scheme for universal socialisation of industry, asking why miners and railwaymen should be specially privileged. The Webbs begged him not to be in such a hurry." The dispute between "right" and "left", as Mrs. Cole went on to explain (letter of 8th March), was not about socialisation, on which they were all agreed, but "on the *method* of attaining a socialist society". "Direct action," she said, "in so far as its advocates did not join the Communist party, declined when the slump came and died with the general strike."

This was fortunate for the Labour party which could then

develop free from any taint of Communism. It rejected every application of the new Communist party for affiliation; it passed a resolution in 1925 making Communists ineligible for membership in the Labour party and its associated bodies. But reliance on parliamentary gradualism had its opponents in the party and so a party split developed between "left" and "right".

Later in the nineteen-thirties the intellectuals on the "left", Tawney, Cole and Laski, shocked by the MacDonaldite desertion, impressed their image on Labour's new policy and before the Second World War ended they had the party re-committed to a fully socialistic programme. This was popularly expressed in the 1945 election pamphlet *Let Us Face the Future*, which was intended to show how a first instalment of Clause 4 could be carried out. Some of the intellectual "left" doubted the practicability of parliamentary gradualism and held the idea that Clause 4 could never be implemented without a revolution. Laski in particular was driven by this logic into expressing such extreme revolutionary sentiments that he was singled out for attack in the press—subsequently he brought a libel action which he lost—but the majority held firm to their parliamentary gradualism. So the first phase in the "socialisation of all the means of production, distribution and exchange" was confined to the nationalisation of coal, gas, electricity, railways, road transport, civil aviation, cables and wireless, iron and steel and the Bank of England.

In *Let Us Face the Future* there was a hint of more to come. The Labour party, it said, "is a socialist party and proud of it. Its ultimate purpose at home is the establishment of the socialist commonwealth of Great Britain. But socialism cannot come overnight as the product of a weekend revolution. There are basic industries ripe and over-ripe for public ownership. . . . There are big industries not yet ripe. . . . Labour believes in land nationalisation and will work towards it." But these brave words were quickly forgotten. I remember saying in a speech to the New York State Chamber of Commerce in April 1947, that with the iron and steel Bill "Socialism in Britain had shot its bolt". American bankers at that time were convinced that Britain was turning Communist: they could hardly believe their ears when they heard this prophecy. But it was true. The old capitalist system was changed into a mixed economy of public and private sectors (with the public responsible for over 30% of the national product) but private enterprise remained the real driving force in the economy.

The truth is that the great socialistic fandango of 1945 ended in anti-climax. By 1951 nothing that could be recognised as socialism was established except the national health service and the new towns. Aneurin Bevan apart, a tired lot of right-wing Ministers, exhausted by their war-time offices, tried ineffectively to implement a radical programme of social change which had not been carefully thought out and prepared beforehand—and they made a hash of it. By 1947—that "annus horrendus" as Dalton described it[1]—they had lost their drive. They left unchanged the social status of the workers. The rich had become richer, the privileged no less powerful. The "commanding heights of the economy" were still in the hands of the vested interests in the City. Nothing in fact was done to lay the foundations of the promised planned, egalitarian socialist State. Instead of closing the division in their ranks the leaders left a deep party split (Aneurin Bevan, Harold Wilson and John Freeman resigning from the Government) and by failing to win over the trade unions to their wage restraint policy—because they tackled dividend limitation too late—they allowed the working class once again to feel disillusioned and alienated from society as a whole. It was a sad sequel to the overwhelming popular vote of 1945. When Hartley Shawcross made his famous victory cry: "We are the masters now!" he implied that the submerged working mass need no longer look upon the ruling clique as "them" but "us". We were now, he imagined, all one society. Alas, his colleagues in 1951 left it as hopelessly split as it was before.

[1] *High Tide and After; memoirs, 1945-1960* by Hugh Dalton, Muller, 1962.

SEVEN

# FRUSTRATION AND DISILLUSIONMENT, 1945-51: DALTON

I CAN WELL UNDERSTAND the state of disillusionment which befell the working class after a Labour Government had been in office for nearly six years. I was feeling pretty disillusioned myself. This was due to my personal disenchantment over Hugh Dalton, whose accession to power at the Treasury had filled me originally with such high hopes. In the nineteen-thirties Vaughan Berry, a bill broker employed by the Union Discount Company, and I had formed a dining club among our City friends—it was called XYZ—for the express purpose of inviting the Labour leaders to dinner in order to educate them about the facts of life in the City. We found them ill-informed and suspicious of the City institutions. The Stock Exchange, the hub of the capital market, which is a vital part of the mechanism of the capitalist system and the most efficiently and democractically managed institution in the City, they regarded as a sort of casino. They did not even know the difference between stock-jobbers and stock-brokers. We zealously invited real-life City people to meet them, people who were staunch Conservatives but not unsympathetic to change. We wrote papers and produced statistics. Berry composed a first rough draft for nationalising the Bank of England. I was the specialist on the capital market, having lectured on this subject to the Liberal summer schools when I was working with Keynes and Henderson. Being strongly in favour of a planned economy, I advocated the setting-up of a National Investment Board—as in the old Liberal plan—and was intrigued to find that Dalton lifted my paper and put it almost bodily into a Labour Party policy memorandum which was published in 1934. This broadsheet proposed a National Investment Board "to mobilise our financial resources and guide them into the right channels" (my words) and "advise the Government on a financial plan for the full employment of our people" (his words). In the pamphlet *Let Us Face the Future* the Labour party stressed the importance of "planned investment" and promised that "a National Investment

Board will determine social priorities and promote better financing in private investment".

To my chagrin Dalton dropped the National Investment Board as soon as he arrived at the Treasury. He had been staying with me in the country for the weekend before, discussing some ideas I had put forward, and when I motored him to Great George Street on the Monday morning he had said with a wave of assurance as he slammed the door: "I have got your XYZ papers in my bag and I am going to put them on my desk, press the button for my new slaves and ask them why we should not put them into practice." I found that the slaves became his masters.

The Treasury hierarchs had always been opposed to any outside planning organisation which would detract from their paramount control of the economy. I imagine that Bridges, the then permanent Secretary, who had his finger in every pie, persuaded Dalton that a National Investment Board was unnecessary. Were not five big industries, the main spenders on capital account, to be nationalised? Would this not give the Government a firm enough control of investment? The Treasury already had a "planning branch" (it was merely a co-ordinating committee at bureaucrat level) and would not another Board duplicate the planning machinery already at the Chancellor's disposal? Whatever the arguments were which Bridges used, Dalton ratted on the National Investment Board and thereby abandoned the principles of a planned economy. This convinced me that the decision which Attlee made over lunch-time on 27th July 1945, to reverse the offices which he had offered Dalton and Bevin in the morning had been a grievous mistake.

To placate the planning enthusiasts of his party who had been looking forward to and counting on the promised National Investment Board, and were as upset as I was by its non-appearance, Dalton set up a consultative National Investment Council in 1946 on which he invited me to serve. It was a waste of time. The Council was denied by the Treasury all power, all information, all staff and all dignity. We used to meet in the Chancellor's room for tea and a pleasant chat. Bridges and his bureaucrats used to sit behind the Chancellor in rows, their poker faces alert to see that we did not propose anything revolutionary that might upset the Treasury establishment. The thing was a farce and everyone knew it. No planning of the national investment was ever discussed. Members were invited to give their opinion about any subject that entered their heads—provided it was not about planning investment. We were asked our views, for example, about convertibility. I had written to *The Times* at the beginning of the convertibility crisis (2nd August 1947) urging the immediate suspension of gold shipments (I give an extract from this letter on p. 53). Dalton thundered at me disapprovingly: "I see some of you have been writing to the press"—as if it was any good writing to the Council. As soon as Cripps became Chancellor the Council was abolished. Previously Cripps had been appointed Economics Minister—to the dismay of Bridges who wanted to control everything—but with his translation to No. 11 Downing Street economic as well as financial power became centred once again in the Treasury. (The more so when all these Treasury ministers—Chancellor, Economic Secretary and Finance Secretary—were Wykehamists). Thereafter Bridges slept peacefully at nights, confident that the idea of a planned economy directed by independent experts sitting on a National Investment Board outside and above the Treasury had been killed for his time of office. Indeed, it had. The Treasury firmly retained sole control of the economy thereafter and to this we must attribute the succession of post-war financial and economic crises.

There was another XYZ matter on which Dalton failed to live up to his promises and left many others beside Berry and myself sadly disillusioned. This was over the nationalisation of the Bank of England. We had found Labour politicians before 1945 constantly talking of how they would seize "the commanding heights of the economy". This was a Leninist phrase and sounded well when suitably intoned on political platforms before an audience of comrades. We had tried to explain to them that "the commanding heights of the economy" were all to be found within the square mile of the City clustered round and about the Bank of England. We fondly imagined that when they had got control of the Bank they would appoint a technocrat Governor outside politics who was experienced in the monetary management of a mixed economy, that they would restrict the Court of the Bank to technical experts and that they would remove the part-time bankers or merchant directors who, later on, were to give their amateur selves away at the Bank Rate Tribunal. We also expected that they would take power for the Bank to issue and enforce clear directives to the directors of other banks, perhaps requiring Government representation on the boards of the banks so "directed". This was our conception of the practical way in which the money system of the country could be brought under proper public control.

The mistake we made was to suppose that we were dealing with men who knew what they were up against. It became clear that they were either unwilling to make a radical change or were ignorant of the way in which it could be effected. Obviously a true radical like Aneurin Bevan would have turned the old Establishment out and put his own men in. This might have had bizarre results, but what Dalton did was really laughable. First, he asked the existing Governor of the Bank, Lord Catto of Morgan Grenfell, to stay on because he was such a nice friendly chap who had risen up from the ranks. Then he reduced the Court from twenty-four to sixteen and took power to appoint only four of them each year. (He retained the prominent directors who had been associated with the worst disasters of Montagu Norman.) Later, when Dalton had gone, Cripps gave up trying to appoint four Labour supporters each year and accepted as a matter of course the nominations put up to him by the Governor. They were mainly old Etonians. And the Governor he chose, Cobbold, was the protégé of Montagu Norman, the very man who had given Dalton hopelessly wrong advice over convertibility.

I believe that Dalton was blinded partly by ignorance of the way in which the City Establishment worked, partly by conceit over his success in the nationalisation debate, partly by hatred of the left-wing intellectuals like Laski. In his autobiography he wrote: "Once in some Left Book Club circles I had listened to the tedious theory that the capitalists would resist, if necessary by force, a socialist government which would try to nationalise the Bank of England or anything else. Impatiently I had replied: Make me Chancellor of the Exchequer and give me a good Labour majority in Parliament and I will undertake the nationalisation of the Bank of England over a dinner party. And now no dinner party had been necessary: only tea for two." Of course Lord Catto would not resist, or any of his capitalist friends, because they knew that Dalton intended no revolution in the City, planned no real change in the management of the Bank and had no real wish to upset the financial Establishment or undermine the subtle power it exercised through its interlocking bank directorships. It would have been very different if a real revolution had been intended. So Dalton had not made a fool of Laski: he had made a fool of himself. And to many of his left-wing supporters he had betrayed the socialist revolution.

The Act of Nationalisation of the Bank of England was the first of the great measures of socialisation intended to implement Clause 4—and the worst drafted. Dalton called it a "stream-lined socialist statute" but it was stream-lined with ambiguities. As a result of its own obscure Clause 4[1] the Governor and his new Court regarded themselves as an autonomous public board, managing their own affairs independently of Parliament and Treasury! Under this Clause no direction could be given to the Bank *except after consultation with the Governor*, who would, of course, be opposed to any direction. As for directions to the joint stock banks these were to emanate from the Bank, not from the Treasury, and therefore were not likely to emanate at all. As no sanctions were attached to them they could in any case be safely ignored. In fact, no directions have ever been given to this day, partly because, as Cobbold explained at the Radcliffe inquiry, no one was able legally to define a bank.[2]

The Radcliffe Committee was later to report that the Bank had laid "mistaken stress" upon those provisions of the Act which concerned "the affairs of the Bank." The Bank witnesses had told them that in the Governor's opinion "the affairs of the Bank were the fixing of Bank rate, the management of the money market and the management of the issue department's portfolio". The Radcliffe Committee did not agree. They rejected the view expressed by more than one official witness that the public interest required that the central bank should be assured complete political independence. I well remember Macmillan saying to Robert Boothby and myself when he was Chancellor of the Exchequer in 1956—in an interview he gave us on a memorandum I had written—that the Bank of England had become far more independent since it had been nationalised. Nobody, he said, could now sack the Governor or his officials, being

[1] See extract on pp. 52-53.

[2] Writing in the *Fabian Journal* in 1958 Dalton still imagined that the power to issue directives to the banks existed! No directions will ever need to be issued, he said, for it is only necessary to hint at the power. Could he have understood the Act?

civil servants, and the Governor was no longer amenable to political influence. In the old days, he added, you could always influence Montagu Norman if you got him to dine alone and locked all the doors.

*Clause 4 of the Bank of England Act, 1964*

4. (1) The Treasury may from time give such directions to the Bank as, after consultation with the Governor of the Bank, they think necessary in the public interest.

(2) Subject to any such directions, the affairs of the Bank shall be managed by the court of directors in accordance with such provisions (if any) in that behalf as may be contained in any charter of the Bank for the time being in force and any byelaws made thereunder.

(3) The Bank, if they think it necessary in the public interest, may request information from and make recommendations to bankers, and may, if so authorised by the Treasury, issue directions to any banker for the purpose of securing that effect is given to any such request or recommendation:

Provided that:

(a) no such request or recommendations shall be made with respect to the affairs of any particular customer of a banker; and

(b) before authorising the issue of any such directions the Treasury shall give the banker concerned, or such person as appears to them to represent him, an opportunity of making representations with respect thereto.

(4) If, at any time before any recommendations or directions are made or given in writing to a banker under the last foregoing subsection, the Treasury certify that it is necessary in the public interest that the recommendations or directions should be kept secret, and the certificate is transmitted to the banker together with the recommendations or directions, the recommendations or directions shall be deemed, for the purpose of section two of the Official Secrets Act, 1911, as amended by any subsequent enactment, to be a document entrusted in confidence to the banker by a person holding office under

His Majesty; and the provisions of the Official Secrets Acts, 1911 to 1939, shall apply accordingly.
(5) Save as provided in the last foregoing subsection, nothing in the Official Secrets Acts, 1911 to 1939, shall apply to any request, recommendations or directions made or given to a banker under subsection (3) of this section.
(6) In this section the expression "banker" means any such person carrying on a banking undertaking as may be declared by order of the Treasury to be a banker for the purposes of this section.

*Extract from letter to* The Times *of August 2nd 1947*

"Sir. Only $1,000,000,000 of the American loan is left. The accelerated rate of drawings—$700,000,000 this month—points to only one thing—a flight from "free" sterling. This must be stopped at once. We did not borrow from America to provide foreign countries with dollars but our workpeople with food and our factories with raw materials. If we are to survive as a great trading nation we cannot allow our last reserves of gold and dollars to disappear down the drain of a convertibility clause in the American Financial Agreement of December, 1945... Our annual dollar deficit probably exceeds our balance of trade deficit by something like £250,000,000 a year. (This is a cautious guess; as a member of the National Investment Council I have no access to confidential figures.) A flight from "free" sterling at the rate of £750,000,000 a year is unthinkable... I venture to suggest that the Prime Minister should immediately declare that we find the convertibility clause to be unworkable and that we must immediately restrict the conversion of "free" sterling in order to protect our vital dollar reserves, which must be strengthened by drawing the balance of the American loan. In this connexion it would be pertinent for him to point out that the rise in American prices had reduced by about $1,000,000,000 the value of the original loan which we never regarded as adequate to see us through the post-war difficulties.

Nicholas Davenport, *The Athenaeum*, 2 August 1947.

EIGHT

# FRUSTRATION AND DISILLUSIONMENT, 1945-51: MORRISON AND CRIPPS

My own disenchantment over Dalton is not to be compared with the disillusionment which the working class must have felt over nationalisation after six years of Labour party rule. They had been told to prepare for the dawn of the socialist millennium but nationalisation turned out to be a very different affair from the socialism which they had expected. It appeared to them merely an alternative system of management. Public ownership was, so to speak, downgraded from socialism to managerialism and the only difference between the old managers and the new was that the old were tophatted capitalists and the new bowler-hatted bureaucrats. What is more, the attitude of the new bureaucrats to the workers was no more humanly sympathetic and understanding than that of the old proprietors. The Acts of nationalisation made no change whatsoever in the social status of the workers, for they continued to be treated as "inferior class" citizens liable to be dismissed on a week's notice regardless of their years of service. Nothing came of the old boast in one of the party memoranda that "Labour stands for democracy in industry and for the rights of the workers, both in the public and private sectors, to full consultation on all the vital decisions of management, especially those affecting conditions of work." The new managers of the public boards were not disposed to have any nonsense of shop-floor democracy. To knock this into the workers' heads the Government invariably chose a retired army general to fill the chairman's seat. When the miners in South Wales had General Sir Reade Godwin-Austin foisted on their south-western division they called the N.C.B., the "New Capitalist Bloody Board".

Herbert Morrison had rightly insisted that the public boards should be composed of men technically qualified and competent to do the job, as his London Transport Board had been. But there his imagination stopped. The son of a policeman of working-class origin, he had been running the London County

Council and had little understanding of the aspirations of the industrial worker. He had made good himself and as far as he was concerned there was not much room at the top for the rank and file. He did not appreciate that industrial workers wanted to be treated like human beings with normal ambitions, to be given a contract of service like salaried employees, to be guaranteed compensation if jobs became redundant through no fault of their own, to be provided in that event with training for another job and to be assured that the more ambitious among them could be sent to college to be trained for more highly skilled work and perhaps for managerial duties.

Morrison is not alone to be blamed. He and all his colleagues lacked the imagination to see what the industrial hour required in terms of human understanding. Obviously the Labour nationalisation programme should have provided for an industrial charter for the workers. This charter should have laid it down that all manual workers must have a contract of service entitling them to a month's notice in the event of termination through redundancy with compensation payable at the rate of, say, one week's pay for every year of service. The charter should also have provided for joint consultation committees in every factory and business employing more than a certain number of workers and for re-training and educational facilities to fit displaced workers for other jobs. The failure to offer a charter of industrial rights along these lines was another step in the estrangement of the working class. It suggested that a Labour Government was not interested in raising their social status.

The next shock, making disillusionment even more painful, was the realisation that under the so-called "socialisation" programme the rich were becoming richer far more quickly than the poor were becoming less poor. In a dynamic society a policy of expansion will always tend to make the go-ahead enterpreneur acquire wealth more rapidly than anyone else but there was a technical reason why the programme of nationalisation gave him a special boost. When industries are nationalised and not confiscated the owners rightly receive fair compensation in the form of Government bonds and as these bonds can be cashed on the excellent capital market which the City provides the holders are given a liquidity which they never previously enjoyed. The result in 1945-51 was that the expropriated were able to turn a lot of unsaleable coal shares, railway stock and local gas shares into cash for reinvestment in far more profitable industries. I can give the figure of the monetary uplift which the former proprietors received. At the various issue prices of the nationalisation stocks it came to nearly £3,000 million. When realised and re-invested in the right "growth" industries, provided the individual companies were wisely chosen, this huge sum could easily have been doubled in ten years. Capital in liquid form has always been more valuable to the moneyed class than income. This is a platitude in the City but it must have come as a shock to the innocent socialist who had imagined that nationalisation was intended to deprive the capitalist of a productive asset and secure a wider distribution of wealth.

While the rich were quietly inflating their wealth it began to dawn on the working class that the Labour Government was determined not only to restrain the rise in their wages but to add to the indirect taxation they bore. Dalton had warned them that "the purchase tax has come to stay and must help to pay the bill for social betterment"[1] and in his fourth and last budget had sharply raised the scales all round. A much more austere Cripps had been left to deal with wage restraint.

There was an element of tragedy in this story, for not only had Labour agreed for the best of reasons to a wages policy of restraint in the coalition White Paper of 1944, but it could not possibly have avoided wage restraint in 1945-51 when the war had left an appalling shortage of goods. It was the classic condition for the "demand-pull" type of inflation. In the White Paper of January 1947, written under Dalton's authority as Chancellor, it was revealed that the total amount of incomes after tax in 1946 was well over £7,000 million while the value of goods and services available was only about £6,000 million. Any rise in wages adding to the excess demand would merely have served to create more bottlenecks in the production process and to *reduce* supply. Stocks of all materials were so low that factories often had to close for a period to allow them to build up. In the bitterly cold winter of 1947 stocks of coal actually ran out and Shinwell, Minister of Fuel, had to tell the House of Commons that a large part of industry would have to shut down until the weather improved.

In February 1948, another white paper on *Personal Incomes Costs and Prices*[2] was issued on the authority of Cripps, who had

[1] Quoted in *High Tide and After*. [2] Cmnd. 7321.

become Chancellor in the previous October after Dalton's autumn budget indiscretion (a trivial lapse due to nervous and mental exhaustion). This White Paper proposed that increases in costs due to higher wages should actually be disallowed for purposes of price control. It baldly declared:

> It is essential that there should be no further general increase in the level of personal incomes without at least a corresponding increase in the volume of production. . . . Until more goods and services are available for the home market there is no justification for any general increase of individual money incomes. Such an increase will merely raise costs of production without making more goods available and so can only have an inflationary effect. . . . To sum up, if general increases in profits, salaries or wages take place without more goods being made available no one can obtain any real benefit except the black market operator.

This was the strongest incomes warning so far issued by the Treasury and it could only have come from a Chancellor with the moral stature of Stafford Cripps. The trade unions had at first co-operated with Cripps but they were always careful to leave loopholes for a subsequent rise in incomes. For example, at a conference of trade union executives called by the T.U.C. "restraint" was agreed to provided that the claims of those "below a reasonable standard of subsistence" were met and that "essential differentials" were maintained. This proviso let in a flood of claims although the White Paper of February 1948 had expressly warned the nation that a claim for an increase in wages or salaries "must be considered on its national merits and not on the basis of maintaining a former relativity between different occupations and industries". In the budget of April 1948 Cripps exacted the "special levy" on capital to prove to the workers that he was demanding a sacrifice from the rich as well as from the poor. But the Labour party's Conference which followed in May 1948 failed to give him any firm support. This was not surprising, seeing that in real terms wage rates in 1948 were not higher but lower than in 1947. At the next conference in June 1949, Cripps had to reply to a trade union attack that the wage restraint policy had reacted "unfairly against the workers and has had little or no effect on the control of profits". In an almost religious fervour Cripps replied: "It is not more money which we want, it is more goods; we want our money to be worth more in purchasing power and not less. Our party has always insisted . . . upon the supremacy of moral values."

But Cripps could not import his moral fervour into the hearts of his trade union colleagues. Wage costs in money terms went on rising and although (relative to American prices) British export prices were only slightly higher than in 1937-38, a speculative raid on sterling developed—the Americans putting out a rumour that the £ was to be devalued—and the gold reserves fell.

Cripps had set his face against devaluation. "Unhappily", writes Douglas Jay in *Hugh Gaitskell, 1906 to 1963*[1] (page 94): "Stafford Cripps, worn down by persistent overwork into worsening health, was forced in July 1949 to retire for two months' convalescence abroad just at the moment when economic opinion had become almost unanimous that devaluation to about $3.00 in September was the right, and indeed almost the only, remedy. In this situation, when every opportunity for delay and confusion existed, Hugh Gaitskell, who had been given part authority for Treasury policy under the Prime Minister in Cripps' absence, made up his mind, clearly and decisively, what needed to be done, convinced the doubters, including the Chancellor himself while abroad, and supervised all the arrangements . . . with remarkable efficiency and absolute secrecy." This disclosure suggests that the clear-headed Gaitskell had intended writing down the £ to $3.00 but that Cripps, stricken by ill-health and his judgment impaired, got into a panic when he returned to the Treasury in September (Gaitskell going to the Ministry of Fuel) and overdid it with a devaluation of 30%—from $4.03 to $2.80. There is no doubt that this was excessive and in so far as it pushed up domestic prices it was particularly harmful to the interests of the working population, which no one seemed to have time to consider. But nerves at the Treasury were frayed and Cripps was not the only one whose judgment was impaired.

In his budget speech of April 1950, Cripps had to admit the breakdown of wage restraint. "It was not possible", he said, "to continue indefinitely the rigidity of the policy in regard to personal incomes which was initiated immediately after the devaluation of sterling." By the summer prices were rising

[1] Ed. W. T. Rodgers, Thames and Hudson, 1964.

and wages following suit. Thereafter the trade unions paid little attention to the policy of restraint and passed a resolution against the maintenance of it at their Brighton conference in September 1950.

It is interesting to find Sir Roy Harrod making this trenchant comment in his summing up of the economy in this period:

"The large and cumulative rise in the cost of living, which followed the devaluation, made it absolutely impossible to maintain this wages pause. It might be objected that by stern discipline wages could have been held down; but this is quite unrealistic; by no reckoning could it be supposed that, after ten years of severe austerity, British wage-earners could be expected to have their real standard of living reduced by 10% or more. Discipline might have availed to keep the wages pause in being in relation to a moderate devaluation, but not in relation to one which was so grossly excessive."[1]

If only Cripps had looked less like a gaunt vegetarian saint and more like a frustrated *bon viveur* the workers might have accepted austerity from him as a necessary forerunner of an affluent society to come—in which case we could have had a more sensible and better timed devaluation—but the trouble was that he offered no promise of relief, no prospect of expansion, in fact, no policy of economic hope at all. All he seemed to offer was austerity for austerity's sake.

What Cripps had done was simply to bottle up the wages steam in the industrial boilerhouse. And he had bottled it up for the time quite effectively. From February 1948 to August 1950 wage rates had risen by 5% but retail prices by 8%. The table on the next page shows that the rise in weekly wage rates from 1946 to 1951 was hardly more than was required to offset the rise in retail prices.

In this period the index of average weekly earnings rose by 30% and in real terms by a little over 6%. In other words, under six years of socialism the workers had to work a great deal of overtime to improve their standard of living by a tiny 1% a year.

Gaitskell, having decided to spatchcock a rearmament programme into an over-extended economy, perforce carried on the Crippsian policy of restraint when he became Chancellor

[1] *The British Economy* by Sir Roy Harrod, McGraw-Hill Book Company, 1963.

in October 1950. He had hoped to secure trade union support for wage restraint even at this late hour by introducing a bill to limit dividends which he announced in July 1951, but the Government fell before it could be carried through. The final collapse came with a bitter and squalid controversy between Gaitskell as Chancellor and Bevan as rebel over paltry charges in the national health service for false teeth and spectacles. By this time the rank and file of the trade unions could see little difference between their Labour leaders and the old ruling clique.

INDEX: AVERAGE 1955 = 100

| | *Weekly wage rates* | *Retail prices* | *Real weekly wage rates* |
|---|---|---|---|
| 1946 | 63·6 | 67·3 | 94·5 |
| 1947 | 66·4 | 67·7 | 98·1 |
| 1948 | 69·9 | 72·1 | 96·9 |
| 1949 | 71·7 | 74·2 | 96·6 |
| 1950 | 73·1 | 76·5 | 95·6 |
| 1951 | 79·3 | 83·5 | 95·0 |

(Source: Ministry of Labour statistics; *National Institute Economic Review*, No. 15.)

NINE

# WAS 1951 ANOTHER 1931?

IT MAY SEEM strange that the overwhelming vote for socialism which the Labour Party secured in 1945 should have been followed by a marginal victory for Conservative free enterprise in 1951. It was due, as I have suggested, to the feeling of frustration and disillusionment which swept over the working class after six years of Labour rule. A Labour Government, they must have reasoned, had failed to turn a capitalist society into a socialist one; so why not vote for a party which knew how to make a capitalist society work? Some simple argument of that kind may have helped to tip the scales in favour of the Tories. Yet there was more behind the rejection of Attlee than that. The workers must have felt that in high finance 1951 had been another 1931. As far as they could understand it, there had been a similar exchange crisis, a similar attack on wages and a similar cut in public assistance—this time in the health service. Attlee did not, of course, betray his colleagues, but he threw up the political sponge. He had no doubt been a tough and courageous Prime Minister, enforcing consumer rationing and controls long enough to allow the export trade to treble between 1946 and 1951, but his courage failed him, as it did MacDonald and Snowden, when a new financial crisis blew up. Yet he had reached a point in our remarkable post-war economic recovery when he himself could have promised the end of austerity after he had solved the immediate financial crisis.

This point is worth elaborating. The worst problem which the Labour Government faced on taking office was the balance of payments. At the end of the war a White Paper had given an inventory of our war-time losses—one-third of our merchant marine sunk, one-half of our export trade lost to the Americans, £1,000 million of overseas investments sold and a load of debt (£3,500 million) incurred abroad—mostly in the sterling area. The authors of this horror paper, in which Keynes had a hand, forecast terrible difficulties ahead for the balancing of payments. (Keynes had his eye, of course, on an American loan.) Our "invisible" account had become a minus quantity (against

£332 million plus annually from 1935 to 1938) and our attenuated export trade was paying for only three-quarters of our imports. So Dalton went begging for a dollar loan and after a prickly negotiation Keynes secured one for $3,750 million (Canada generously following with $1,250 million). These "billions" of dollars tided the Government over its difficult period of deficit trading in 1946-47. Indeed, we would have been "sunk" without it, for in 1947, when the outer sterling area was running a heavy adverse balance with the dollar area, the total deficit on our balance of payments had risen to the alarming total of £553 million.

Now our trade recovery was far more rapid than the sponsors of the American loan had expected. In 1948 the export trade had already surpassed the Government target of "75% above pre-war". Total exports were then £1,604 million against only £533 million in 1938. From 1948 to 1950 the net pluses from shipping, from interest and dividends and from "other credits" also began to build up steadily, so that the "invisible" account actually produced an average surplus in the period of £282 million a year. (In real terms this was only equivalent to about £140 million—at 1938 prices—but was none the less encouraging.) In the last quarter of 1949 exports had the stimulus of the devaluation in sterling but this should not be exaggerated. As an Oxford economist correctly pointed out, the actual depreciation of sterling for practical trade purposes (so many imports coming from and so many going to the sterling area) was only about 18%.[1] However, by 1950 the export trade had been firmly re-established. In that year it reached the then staggering total of £2,254 million against only £920 millions in 1946. (Today it is over £4,000 million.)

For this achievement the Labour Government deserves high praise. It conducted a lively export propaganda—"Export or Die" was its slogan—and made the business world export conscious. And it took special measures to boost exports by the strict control and allocation of materials. For example, the motor industry only got its supply of steel on condition that it would export a high proportion of its output (75% at one stage) while the pottery industry was directed to export everything except a minimum of miserable utility articles and spoilt ware. The nation accepted this harsh austerity in consumer

[1] Miss P. Ady in *The British Economy in the 1950's*, Clarendon Press, Oxford, 1962.

goods and took pride in the splendid recovery in the balance of payments. The first overall surplus on our international trading account had actually appeared in 1948 with the tiny plus figure of £7 million. But by 1950 the surplus had reached £297 million. For the first time since the war we were really solvent. It was a magnificent achievement. But it went to the Labour Government's head. In the autumn of that year they were rash enough to renounce further use of Marshall Aid which could have been carried on for another twelve to fifteen months. The Korean war had broken out in July 1950 and the prospect of a rise in Government spending overseas should have made them less optimistic.

The huge deficit on the international trade account which blew up in 1951 and frightened the Labour Government out of office—the deficit amounted in the twelve months to £419 million—was due entirely to the £1,110 million jump in imports. There was no mystery about it. Our international account turns on slender margins and occasionally we are bound to have thumping great import bills and deficits. In the case of 1951 the sharp rise in imports—from £2,390 to £3,501 million—was caused partly by the stocking-up required for the rearmament programme and the domestic trade expansion, partly by the worsening of the terms of trade superimposed on the devaluation mark-up of sterling prices. The Korean war had brought about a sharp rise in commodity prices and within the space of twelve months the price level of our imports had risen by nearly 50%. The worsening balance of payments could have been countered—as it was by the Tory Chancellor in November 1951—by stricter control over imports, that is, by revoking open general licences and imposing import quotas. Obviously it had been a mistake to remove in 1950 the extra import restrictions which had been imposed at the time of the devaluation. In July 1951 they had to be re-imposed and Douglas Jay informs us[1] that they would have been followed by other restrictions in the autumn. But it was left to a new Conservative Government to deal with the final solution of the balance of payments crisis. Attlee had funked it.

My conclusion is that the Attlee Government could have solved this financial crisis if Labour had been a united party. Gaitskell's first and only budget (April 1951) was a courageous

[1] In *Hugh Gaitskell, 1906-1963*.

attempt to impose sufficient taxation to meet the £700 million increase in defence expenditure[1] but he over-taxed the loyalty of Bevan and Wilson when he tried to extract a little money from teeth and spectacles in the national health scheme.

Admittedly there was some foreign nervousness over the £, which the City was quick to exaggerate, but should Attlee have capitulated to the City? No doubt he had been unnerved by the convertibility debacle in 1947 when £152 million had been lost from the gold reserves in a rash attempt to honour the American loan agreement, but is it always going to be left to financial rumour-mongers in New York, London and Zurich to turn out a British Labour Government when they feel inclined? Did not the I.M.F. exist to help countries in temporary balance of payment trouble over their exchange crises? Attlee may, of course, have felt that Gaitskell was trying to do the impossible (as Bevan argued) when he imposed a huge rearmament programme on an already over-extended economy, but having agreed with Gaitskell to give rearmament priority and "hang" the balance of payments he should not have been surprised at an exchange crisis. He should have faced it and taken the obvious steps to deal with it. As soon as the Tories got into office drastic import restrictions were imposed and Churchill announced that the £1,250 million rearmament programme (part of the three-year £4,700 million plan) would have to be scaled down. It is interesting to note that the Conservatives solved this balance of payments crisis without a high Bank rate.[2]

It may seem strange that the Labour Government throughout its tenure of office should have pursued a finance-capitalist policy in regard to sterling and the balance of payments. The truth is that in these financial matters it had an inferiority complex. It accepted without question the advice of the establishment in the higher Civil Service which was trained and rooted in finance-capitalism. It never dreamt of re-thinking the external or sterling problem in the light of the long-term interests of the working population. It was a great misfortune

[1] Gaitskell's budget put 6*d.* on the income tax (making it 9*s.* 6*d.* in the £), doubled the purchase tax on motor-cars, radio and domestic electrical equipment, raised the profits tax on distributed profits from 30% to 50% and suspended the initial allowances.

[2] Bank rate was raised from 2% to 2½% in November 1951 and to 4% in March 1952.

that in the critical financial years the three ministers at the Treasury were all Wykehamists. There is a natural intellectual affinity between Wykehamists and the higher Civil Service amounting almost to mutual adoration of brains. Cripps, Gaitskell and Jay all adored their civil servants. As Jay once said, giving us all a hollow laugh: "The man in Whitehall knows best." Richard Crossman in a brilliant analysis of this episode wrote: "If in 1931 the MacDonald government was killed by the aristocratic embrace, in 1951 the Attlee government quietly expired in the arms of the Whitehall Establishment."[1] Crossman was a Wykehamist of a different order.

Labour party loyalists have never forgiven Attlee for allowing the fruits of the austerity period—the necessary prelude to recovery—to be gathered in by their political opponents. The subsequent derationing and consumer plenty which followed helped the Conservatives to build up their popularity in the country and win three elections in a row. But much the same bounty could have been handed out in the next few years by any competent government which understood elementary economics and knew how to handle finance.

[1] *New Statesman*, 19th April, 1963.

TEN

# CONSERVATIVE CYNICISM

UNDER THE Conservative régime the acquisitive society flowered into full bloom. The acquisitive instinct being universal, everyone was on the make. In the beginning both sides of the divided nation welcomed the change of government—the workers because there was no Crippsian conscience to make them feel guilty about their wage claims, the employers because controls were being dismantled and they were now free not only to make more money for their companies and distribute more dividends to their share-holders but to get down to the serious business of increasing their own private wealth. The rise in wages did not worry them. In periods of full employment they could easily pass that on to the consumer in higher prices. What was important for them was the rise in the market value of their equity shares which could at any time be cashed in for a tax-free capital profit. As soon as their companies were free once again to distribute share bonuses and to raise fresh capital by "rights" issues the share markets were able to shake off their socialist freeze and show what a policy of economic growth meant in terms of Stock Exchange prices.

From June 1952 to July 1955, there was, in fact, a breathtaking boom in equity shares during which prices more than doubled. The *Financial Times* index of industrial ordinary shares rose from 103 to 224. There followed nearly three years of ups and downs and then the equity market staged another spectacular boom, the *F.T.* index rising from 154 to 366 between 1958 and May 1961. After falling to 253 (June 1962) it regained 366 by August 1964. This advance of 255% was equivalent to a capital gain in real terms of 183%. Add the net dividends received in real terms and the gain becomes about 225%.

Stock Exchange statistics give a fair idea of the increase in private wealth under the Conservative régime. In April 1951, the market value of all securities (Government bonds, fixed interest stocks and equity shares combined) was £26,900 million—only slightly higher than it was in April 1946. By April 1964 it had reached a total of £59,841 million. The gross dividends and interest received in these thirteen years amounted to £18,536 million. It may therefore be assumed that the average rich man more than doubled his capital in the thirteen years to April 1964, without having to exercise his brains. If, however, he had invested his capital shrewdly in equity shares or made use of the professional brains available in the City he would have trebled it.[1]

The workers, reading about this furious Stock Exchange boom in the headlines of their popular paper, naturally became more and more cynical about the slogan "Conservative freedom works". Some of them joked: If Conservative freedom works, why should we? They assumed, of course, that this gave them freedom to go on demanding higher and higher wages. "In a free for all", Frank Cousins sagely remarked, "labour is part of the all." From the next table it will be seen that the average male manual worker over twenty-one was able in the period from April 1951 to December 1963 to push up his weekly pay packet from 160/- to 335/-. This was equivalent in real terms to a rise of 50%.

AVERAGE WEEKLY EARNINGS OF MALE MANUAL WORKERS OVER TWENTY-ONE

| | *Weekly earnings* | *Consumer price index (1954 = 100)* | *Weekly earnings in real terms* |
|---|---|---|---|
| 1938 | 69/- | 41 | 168/- |
| Jan. 1946 | 114/- | 69 | 165/- |
| April 1951 | 160/- | 91 | 176/- |
| April 1962 | 311/- | 123 | 253/- |
| April 1963 | 322/- | 125 | 258/- |
| Dec. 1963 | 335/- | 127 | 264/- |

(Sources: London and Cambridge Economic Service and *National Institute Economic Review*.)

Such were the workers' rewards under the Conservative régime. They were not particularly striking. Only occasionally was a spectacular success won in a wages dispute. For example, in 1957, when the Government was politically weak after the Suez debacle, the railwaymen won a resounding victory over

[1] The figures are taken from the statistics published annually by the Stock Exchange and include new issues during each year.

wage restraint and this was followed, after a nation-wide strike, by the engineers and shipbuilders. But in the following year Frank Cousins was beaten in his bus strike All this time the workers must have felt that they could not relax in their struggle to keep their wages ahead of the rise in prices. A gain in their real standard of living of only 50% in about thirteen years does not stand up against the rise of 183% (in real terms) in the value of equity shares (225% with net dividends added) which the owners of capital enjoyed. With the purchasing power of the 1951 £ down to 13*s.* 6*d.* by 1964 the workers must have felt that they had fought a losing battle. And they never managed to win a larger slice of the national income. Their share remained at a little over 42% throughout the Conservative régime.

DIVISION OF THE NATIONAL INCOME

| | *1938* | *1948-51* | *1952-55* | *1956-59* | *1960-62* |
|---|---|---|---|---|---|
| Wages | 39·9% | 43·4% | 43·0% | 42·7% | 42·0% |
| Salaries[1] | 18·9% | 21·4% | 21·9% | 23·4% | 25·4% |

[1] Salaries include directors' fees; wages exclude employers' contribution and Forces' pay.

(Source: National Income and Expenditure Blue Books.)

Of course, the bigger pay-packet seemed wonderful to the worker's family and it encouraged them to buy their household amenities ahead by the use of the ingenious techniques of hire purchase and consumer credits. Whenever the financial controls were eased, these "never-never" facilities were quickly and widely extended. This spurt in better living in the home undoubtedly deceived the working man's family into thinking that they were much better off than in fact they were. This may explain why the Conservative Party won victory so easily at the two subsequent general elections and why the right wing of the Labour Party tried so hard to dissociate itself from any formal commitment to socialism in order to win back the votes of the workers who agreed with Macmillan that they "had never had it so good".

As the outward show of affluence grew more splendid in the average worker's home, so the feeling of cynicism grew deeper in his heart. He knew that everyone in this acquisitive society was on the make and that the rich were beating him in the race because they had capital and the expertise to make it grow. So when the opportunity came in 1961 for the trade unions to jump on the bandwagon in Throgmorton Street they did not let this ironic situation pass. Suppressing their disapproval of the capitalist's sordid pursuit of material wealth, they participated in a unit trust formed under the auspices of a City merchant bank to invest trade union subscriptions in "growth" equity shares. Lord Longford gave it more than his moral blessing by accepting the chairmanship. A richly sardonic touch was to invite on the board of this unit trust a financial journalist who had spent his years declaiming against the inflationary implications of the annual round of wage claims. In Rome you must obviously do as the Romans do, and, better still, get a guide to show you how. In this case the financial journalist would be the guide picking out the shares which would offer the best hedge against the potential cost-inflation caused by his trade union colleagues. Apparently the workers had no objection to tax-free capital gains. After all, when one of them in a million could win a few hundred thousand pounds out of the football pools they would be very angry if the pay-out were not tax-free.

Some of the Tories were sensitive to the charge that in an expanding economy with a booming Stock Exchange the man with the capital must obviously do better for himself than the worker without capital. So a "Wider Share Ownership" Committee was formed in 1958 and was active in its propaganda when Maurice Macmillan, son of Harold, was its chairman. It argued that three million shareholders were not enough. It campaigned for a "wider spread in the personal ownership of the wealth of the country". A motion to that effect which it introduced into the House of Commons a few years ago was welcomed by every member of the Establishment except the old-fashioned nationalising Socialists who protested against the coming of the "gambler's State", with its football pools, premium bonds (Harold's invention) and Stock Exchange speculation. Perhaps as a result of the "Wider Share Ownership" campaign the technical facilities which enable a man without capital to acquire equity shares on the instalment plan have been greatly improved. The first savings plan for unit trust holders was introduced ten years ago and today most unit trust managements will take monthly deposits of savings for investments in their units. Some have gone further and offered life assurance as well which allows the investor to secure tax relief on his subscriptions and so acquire his portfolio of equity shares at a discount.[1] But there is no evidence that these ingenious schemes are appealing to the working man. The remarkable growth of unit trusts, whose invested funds have risen from £60 million to £400 million since 1958 suggest that it is the extensive middle class which is eagerly swallowing the bait of the latest advertising. Indeed, the fact that the average holding in unit trusts at the end of May 1964 was £334 is proof of its middle-class appeal. Betting on horses and the football pools remain the chief outlet of the working man's craze for gambling—his only serious attempt at capital accumulation. The miraculous luck of the very few who attain a super-capitalist status overnight on the stake of a few shillings on the pools seems to encourage most working families to endure a lifetime of weekly tries and failures. The fact that these colossal pool winnings remain tax-free has taken the sting out of the Labour attack on Selwyn Lloyd for allowing Stock Exchange gains after six months' incubation to be free of his capital gains tax.[2]

[1] For example the M. & G. advertising quotes an example of £100 saved and invested every year through their unit-trust-life scheme. £3 is deducted for their expenses and £4 for the cost of life assurance. The balance of £93 is invested in the unit portfolio but as the tax relief on the £100 life assurance subscription amounts to £15 10*s.* the net cost of obtaining £93 worth of units is £84 10*s.* 0*d.*

[2] The Capital Gains Tax introduced by Selwyn Lloyd was not a serious attempt to tax capital gains. It was limited to six months on shares (three years on land) and was intended primarily to catch the Stock Exchange professional traders who used to make a daily business of going "in" and "out".

ELEVEN

# A "CLASS WAR" MONETARY POLICY

THE CONSERVATIVE administration realised that a full employment policy without an incomes policy could lead to inflationary pressures and it always appreciated that it could not enforce an incomes policy on an unwilling and uncooperative labour movement. So it decided on two important moves to circumvent trade union demands.

The first was to bring back into use the monetary weapon to reinforce the fiscal, in other words, the manipulation of Bank rate and the control of bank credit both in volume and quality. A monetary deflation, it believed, if applied firmly enough on the right occasions, could teach the trade unions a useful lesson by throwing men out of work, as was done in the 'twenties and 'thirties, if their wage demands became excessive. It was realised that such a policy would have to be drastic to be effective, but it did not seem to occur to any Tory Chancellor that socially it was a dangerous policy. A whole-hogging deflation as ruthlessly carried out as it was by Thorneycroft and Selwyn Lloyd was bound to be regarded by the trade unions as an act of class-war.

The second move was to bring the pressure of public opinion to bear on trade union demands by means of hostile public propaganda. This was to be carried out from 1958 through the reports of a new Council on Prices, Productivity and Incomes which Thorneycroft established, but the plot somewhat miscarried. The Council started with two strongly anti-trade union reports drafted by an austere minded Cambridge economist, Dennis Robertson, who had an obsession about a wage-demand inflation,[1] but it ended with some constructive reports when Robertson had been replaced by a less rigid economist, Phelps-Brown, and the chairman, Lord Cohen, by the more liberal-minded Lord Heyworth. The first two Robertsonian reports only served to make the division between employers and workers sharper than before and, indeed, to anger both sides of our split society. The trade unions, of course, refused to give evidence before a Council which, they thought,

[1] See pages 119 et seq. for a discussion of the various types of inflation.

was only interested in keeping wages down. It was in any case childish to expect the workers to learn the harsh facts of economic life from the lectures of "three wise men" from the professional class—even when they became "three wiser men" on the change in the Council's constitution.

As regards the monetary weapon it has never been proved, as the Radcliffe Committee reminded us, that it is possible to maintain equilibrium in a free economy by the mere use of interest rates and credit controls.[1] Yet Tory Chancellors went on acting as though Bank rate was the hand of an omnipotent God and monetary policy the work of divine magic. The official economic adviser to the Treasury, Sir Robert Hall, even confessed:[2] "There is still a tendency to speak in magical rather than scientific terms of the use of interest rates and of monetary controls generally. The economy is to be given a potion or dose and wonderful results will follow." A potion or dose of tighter credit, of course, merely drove frustrated borrowers to other sources of credit, foreign as well as domestic, at more expensive money rates[3] which raised the cost of all capital expenditures.

Severe deflationary measures applied to the whole economy by way of dearer money, tighter credit, higher indirect taxes, restrictions on hire purchase trading and cuts in public spending were bound to lead to social friction. Nothing enraged the working class so much as to be told that wage restraint was necessary for price stability and then to find the Government raising prices through higher purchase taxes and rents. This happened again and again and the apparent insanity of it—reminiscent of a Groucho Marx extravaganza—maddened the trade unions as much as its obvious bias against the working class. "Keep prices stable", thundered the Tory Chancellors, and the next day up went Bank rate by 1% and another 10/- was added to the weekly rent of a new Council house. "Don't upset the cost of living", they cried, and with the next budget up went purchase tax on a whole range of household necessities! It was a form of torture calculated to make the mildest

[1] Para. 514 of the Radcliffe Report ran: "When all has been said, our conclusion is that monetary measures cannot alone be relied upon to keep in nice balance an economy subject to major strains from both without and within. Monetary measures can help but that is all."

[2] Sir Robert Hall. "Reflections on the Practical Application of Economics", *Economic Journal*, December 1959, p. 648.

[3] See Radcliffe Committee report paras. 460 and 514.

trade unionist explode into bitter hatred of Conservative financial policy. The end result of this Tory deflation was, of course, a worsening wage-cost inflation. The measures taken to achieve price stability were bound to put prices and wages up.

Such a crazy monetary policy pointed to neurosis. It stemmed from the neurotic attitude of fright adopted by the ruling clique when confronted with the persistent wage claims of the working class. The fright was seen at its worst when Thorneycroft actually confessed that he was prepared to throw men out of work in order "to save the £" and when Selwyn Lloyd denied working people their right to arbitration awards over wage claims.

Many trade unionists were particularly incensed by the imposition of dear money on the local Councils. In 1955 the Conservative Government forced local authorities into the monetary firing line, insisting that they should borrow as far as possible in the open market in their own name and on their own credit. The Public Works Loans Board had to become a lender of last resort and even so at the market rate of interest. The result was appalling. The local authorities were forced into the mortgage market, borrowing on short-term to secure the benefit of the lower rate, but each time there was an exchange crisis and Bank rate was pushed up to 7% to attract "hot money" from abroad the wretched councils had to pay 7½% for funds on seven-day call. The Treasury was in effect making local housing pay the costly bill for buying foreign support of the £!

During the Labour régime the new towns and the local authorities drew money from the Exchequer—the first directly and the second through the Public Works Loan Board—at 3% to 3½%. I well remember it because I was chairman of the finance committee of the Basildon new town when Dalton was Minister of local Government and Planning. We had to revise the rents when Macmillan succeeded him. By 1961 the borrowing rate had doubled and so had the rent of a new Council house. An extra 3½% meant another 40*s.* a week on the rent of a worker's house costing with road and other services £3,000. When Tory Chancellors protested that their dear money was only meant to stop the rise in the cost of living they appeared before the public as liars and hypocrites because they were at the same time putting up the cost of living in a newly built house. The introduction of a "means test" by many Councils was a brave attempt to soften the blow of "dear money" rents on the very poor but it has not been too well received. As for the old houses, the Rent Act caused more social friction than perhaps it deserved but the appearance of the property racketeer on the local scene, pushing frightened tenants out of rent controlled premises by dishonest means, has given Tory landlord legislation a bad name.

I know a working man—now a chauffeur to a Labour peer—who has lived for the past thirty years in a housing slum in North Kensington. All this time he has been fed with promises that the miserable terrace will be pulled down and the tenants properly rehoused. But nothing has been done, except that property racketeers of the Rachman type have moved into action. One can imagine the bitterness of badly housed working people when they see the sky-scraper office blocks and the luxury flats going up in the West End and the City.

Dear money did not, of course, stop the boom in land and property development. Fantastic profits have been made out of it by nimble speculators. More property millionaires have been created in the last ten years than in any other decade in our social history. The refusal of the Conservative Government to apply a licensing system to property development was responsible for an upsurge in office building. There was a strong financial reason for this boom. The rents of offices are paid by companies which can charge them against their gross profits for income tax. So the office property developers had a ready market. But there is no strong financial reason for rehousing the poor. Conservative monetary policy made it much too expensive as a business proposition.

I recall a Sunday afternoon in 1935 when I took Keynes, who was staying with me in the country, to see Cripps at Filkins, his Cotswold home. Cripps told us that when he got into power he would build hundreds of thousands of up-to-date cottages for the agricultural workers and damn the cost and the rate of interest! Keynes was delighted. He had never met a real socialist before who believed passionately in social investment and disbelieved in the relevance of the market rate of interest.

TWELVE

# "STOP-GO-STOP"

THE APPLICATION ON and off of general monetary restraints —popularly known as the "stop-go-stop" policy—has been responsible for the abnormally slow growth of the British economy in the last twelve years. The theory behind the "stop" —the sudden application of the deflationary brakes when the economy is said to be "over-heated" or the balance of payments in deficit—is that it reduces imports, stimulates exports and restores the balance of payments to surplus. But cutting down the home trade does not necessarily stimulate exports in the least. What it does do is to reduce output, raise costs and worsen our competitive position abroad. By denying factories their long production runs it pulls down the productivity of the most efficient expanding industries. It also lessens profitability —the home trade usually allowing a higher margin of profit— and creates a feeling of despondency throughout industry. It makes the businessman feel less inclined to undertake new investment at home or to spend money on improving his sales organisation abroad. And it certainly does not stop the worker from asking for higher wages. Wages went on rising at much the same pace in each period of "Stop". The Conservative reliance on general monetary restraint for economic equilibrium has therefore been fatuous—an irritant to both employers and workers.

The right way to deal with an incipient wage-cost inflation caused by labour pressures in a few over-extended industries is by specific controls applied directly to the trouble spots. There were virtually only two industries capable of setting up a "wage-cost" type of inflation—the building and contracting industry and the motor industry. Over-extension in building and contracting could easily have been averted by a simple licensing system applicable to large building contracts. The motor trades could always be jerked up or slapped down (as indeed they were) by the reduction or increase of the purchase tax on motor-cars. Yet even when total demand and supply in the economy were more or less in balance a Conservative Chancellor would still prefer to deflate everybody in order to deflate a few over-extended industries!

There were thirteen budgets in all under the Conservative régime—four from Butler, one each from Macmillan and Thorneycroft, three from Amory, two from Selwyn Lloyd and two from Maudling. There were twenty-six changes in Bank rate in a little over twelve years. With three pronounced "stops" and four pronounced "go's" it is small wonder that the British economy has not shown steady growth. According to J. C. R. Dow, our greatest expert in these matters, Conservative "budgetary and monetary policy failed to be stabilising and must on the contrary be regarded as having been positively destabilising".[1] It took them twelve years to realise it.

Butler began the first "stop" with his credit restrictions and dearer money in 1951-52. When he came to his first budget in March 1952 there was no "excess demand" in the economy. According to Dow a demand recession was in fact already under way. Yet although income tax was lowered, the petrol duty was increased, food subsidies were reduced and initial allowances were cut in order to slow down investment! De-stocking followed to a larger extent than the Chancellor had anticipated and by 1953 the economy was over-deflated. So the 1953 budget introduced the first "go" with income tax and purchase tax reduced, the excess profits levy removed, the initial allowances restored and building licences liberalised. The 1954 budget was neutral except for the innovation of investment allowances. With a reduction in Bank rate to 3% in May an investment boom naturally got under way. Here was the only occasion under the Tories when it might be said that a "demand-pull" type of inflation was beginning to rear its head. Vacancies became well in excess of the numbers unemployed. Bank rate was accordingly raised from 3% to 3½% in January and to 4½% in February 1955. But instead of applying a "stop" in his budget in April 1955 Butler, with his eye on the coming general election (end of May), took 6*d.* off income tax and gave higher personal allowances. The general election was not unnaturally won. The "stop" was not applied until the autumn budget in October when Butler, confessing his mistake in April, raised both purchase tax and distributed profits tax.

[1] See *The Management of the British Economy, 1945-60*, Cambridge University Press, 1964. Dow was many years in the Treasury's Economic Section and in the National Institute of Economic and Social Research and is now in the Secretariat of the O.E.C.D. in Paris.

By the end of that year Macmillan had replaced a somewhat discredited Chancellor at the Treasury and immediately stiffened up the deflationary policy. Bank rate was raised to 5½% in January 1956, the investment allowances were suspended, public investment cut and hire purchase finance restricted. Macmillan was not unaware of the anti-trade union bias of the Tory "stop" technique. So in an attempt to appear fair to both sides he raised the distributed profits tax to the extreme height of 27½% (undistributed 3%) as well as raising the tobacco duty. This thorough-going deflation brought on the first lengthy period of Tory stagnation. Demand fell for two and a half years until in 1958 the percentage change in the G.N.P. dropped below one, as it did also in 1962.

It was becoming clear even before the Suez debacle that there was going to be a shortage rather than an excess of demand in real terms (the increase in prices having mopped up the increase in incomes). Unfortunately the Chancellor who replaced Macmillan was the "hard money" fanatic Thorneycroft. Instead of consulting his official economic adviser at the Treasury he took the advice of an outside economist, Robbins, who had been preaching the virtues of a hard £ and the need to control the supply of money.[1] Thorneycroft took alarm at the flight of foreign money from sterling which was falsely attributed to a wage-cost inflation. Although he had produced a liberal budget in April 1957, cutting purchase tax and giving higher earned income relief, he had decided by the autumn that he had made a mistake—that the cause of the lack of foreign confidence in sterling was an inordinate rise in wages. It was not: the current trading account was in comfortable surplus. The overseas sterling area was not in dollar deficit. It was a crisis entirely of confidence.

In September 1957, when the country was still enjoying a satisfactory surplus on its balance of payments and when the economic indicators (machine tool orders, factory starts, unfilled vacancies, numbers of unemployed and basic material prices) were all pointing to the early stages of a cyclical decline —the numbers of unemployed had exceeded vacancies for the

[1] Robbins in *Lloyds Bank Review*, April 1958, was to say: "Many are giving more weight to the *push* of costs, less to the *pull* of demand, than I find appropriate. But on one point I hope we shall all be agreed: namely that none of this could happen if there were a sufficiently strong control of the supply of money."

first time for three years—Thorneycroft decided that we must suffer deflation because the £ was in grave danger. So he raised Bank rate to 7% (19th September 1957) in order to protect it. He calmly told bankers at the Mansion House dinner: "If one can regard the economy as an electric current we are ensuring that if the current overloads it, the fuse will not be the £ sterling. The strain must be taken in other areas of policy." This was bad imagery because a growing economy has not, like an electric circuit, a maximum capacity but Thorneycroft wanted to see the volume of employment (which is the workers' livelihood) become the "fuse". Later on, when he informed the Cabinet that as guardian of the £ he must have the last word on Government expenditure he was rebuffed and quickly forced to resign (January 1958). Macmillan, having seen the terrible effects of "hard money" extremism in the nineteen-twenties and thirties was no doubt glad to see him go.

This "hard money" fanatic was succeeded at the Treasury early in 1958 by a mild and genial businessman, Heathcoat Amory. At first he continued the Thorneycroft "stop" but in his April 1958 budget he changed profits tax to a single rate —10%—and so restored business confidence. He went on to reduce Bank rate—down to 4% by November—and to remove the hire-purchase restrictions and the credit squeeze. By allowing banks to extend unlimited consumer credits he started a consumer boom which he failed to control. Between 1958 and 1960 the hire-purchase debt was doubled and bank advances almost doubled. His 1959 budget was positively expansive at the wrong time—income tax cut, purchase tax down, cheaper beer, post-war credits released and investment allowances restored. By this time a dangerous hire-purchase boom had developed in the motor trade. It was possible for a man without any cash to secure a £1,000 motor-car by the simple device of a personal bank loan of £200 for his deposit and a hire-purchase credit for the remainder. This was to cost the hire-purchase finance companies some £50 million in bad debts and put a lot of working-class households into serious trouble.

The 1960 budget of Amory had therefore to apply the "stop". "Demand", said the Chancellor, "seemed to be in danger of outrunning the capacity of the economy." Profits tax was increased to 12½% and before many weeks were out severe credit restrictions and dearer money were imposed. Bank rate had been raised from 4% to 5% in January and was up to 6% by June. Lord Kilmuir wrote in his memoirs:[1] "Many of us had been disappointed by his (Amory's) performance after 1959.... Whether it was merely that the sheer weight of departmental work overwhelmed him in his last months at the Treasury I do not know but it was evident that he had lost his grasp over economic matters." This was evident, too, of his successor, the sado-masochistic Selwyn Lloyd.

By this time the Tory Chancellors might have become a little sensitive about the mistakes of economic judgment which they had made in the "stop-go-stop" technique. They had carried the 1955 boom too far and reversed it too late. From 1956 they held stagnation too long—two and a half years—and in reversing it they pushed consumer spending too far. Then fifteen months afterwards they had to reverse engines again. But that was not all. It was left to Selwyn Lloyd to throw the baby out with the bath water. Under his direction growth stopped, the steel industry worked at 75% capacity and private enterprise investment came to a stand-still.

[1] *Political Adventure: The Memoirs of Lord Kilmuir*, Weidenfeld and Nicolson, 1964.

THIRTEEN

# THE PAY PAUSE AND AFTER

IN THE BEGINNING of their tenure of office the Tory Chancellors had commanded the authors of the annual *Economic Survey* to stop making prognostications of coming trends. And they were particularly careful to make no economic forecasts in their budget speeches. Selwyn Lloyd began to look around for some excuse for estimates going wrong and he found the ideal scapegoat in the trade unions. The misuse of monetary policy under Selwyn Lloyd was to see the culmination of the process, begun in 1925, of alienating the working class through aggressively deflationary monetary measures.

Advised by Frank Lee, the chief of his Treasury hierachs, Selwyn Lloyd decided to have a showdown with the trade unions. There were thirty-five different wage claims pending in the spring of 1961 which could have added £500 million to the national wage bill, so he was determined to put an end once and for all to the wage-cost inflationary spiral. He had been driven to take this drastic decision, partly because he had been told that the increase in incomes in 1961 would be about 50% greater than the increase in output,[1] partly because of the sterling exchange crisis which followed on the huge deficit of £258 million in the 1960 balance of payments. In the first half of 1961 there was a flight of foreign money from London (around £700 million in all) and the £ was saved only by borrowing heavily from the I.M.F. The I.M.F. loan was as usual conditional on steps being taken to end the domestic "inflation" and the Chancellor at once decided upon a 7% Bank rate and a wages pause. To enforce his pay pause he took the unprecedented step of refusing to implement not only the Burnham Committee's award to the teachers but the other arbitration awards currently being made by the Wage Councils. At the same time the Chancellor took power to impose a 10% surcharge on all excise duties—and forthwith exercised it. He will go down in Labour history as the Chancellor who, having raised the standard of living of the surtax-payer (not before it

[1] The increase in incomes in 1961 was about £1,200 million and the increase in output about £800 million.

was due), took steps to lower the standard of living of the working man.

The curious thing was that Selwyn Lloyd had done nothing to prepare either public or trade union opinion for this sudden attack on the time-honoured system of wage negotiation. Almost as an afterthought he had said that a new system of negotiation would have to be devised to secure a more realistic relationship between the rise in wages and the rise in national productivity. He was even prepared for that purpose to accept some State planning of the economy. Out of this ferment of ideas, which no doubt Frank Lee at the Treasury had put into Selwyn Lloyd's bewildered mind, emerged the National Incomes Commission and the National Economic Development Council. The trade unions, of course, would have nothing to do with the first but after some hesitation decided to serve on the second. This point gained, Lloyd dismissed the Council on Prices, Productivity and Incomes which, under Lord Heyworth, had been the first official body to propose a more reasonable wages policy and a planned control of the economy. (He had probably resented their remark that their proposals would call "for a high degree of leadership both on the part of the Government and both sides of industry". He knew that he could not supply it.) A Chancellor who expected the trade unions to co-operate in a wage restraint policy without being offered a *quid pro quo* in the shape of dividend restraint was completely lacking in sensibility. A raising of the profits tax was not enough. And his belated offer of a capital gains tax limited to six months was considered derisory by the trade unions.

In his extraordinarily insensitive approach to the wages problem Selwyn Lloyd had probably been moved by a sado-masochistic impulse to bring suffering on himself and others in order to expiate a sense of guilt. In his view the working class had been sacrificing their country for the sake of their pay-packets and they would have to be taught a lesson by suffering. In a Freudian analysis this sadistic instinct would be an extroversion of his primary masochism and I am sure that his greatest hour came when he received an unexpected letter from his Prime Minister to say that he had been sacked.

When Selwyn Lloyd had gone, both his successor and the Prime Minister endeavoured to offer the trade unions something more tangible in return for wage restraint. Macmillan said in the House of Commons in July 1962: "Restraint on profits and dividends is no less important than on wages and salaries. It is vital that people should not feel that acceptance of restraint on pay meant that someone else got larger profits or dividends. Most economists are agreed that restraint on wages and salaries should be accompanied by a fall in profits. Should that not be so I give this formal pledge that the matter will be dealt with."

Macmillan's strange ideas about profits sprang out of political expediency, not economic understanding. (It will not be forgotten that it was he who displayed his appalling ignorance of business by saying "exporting is fun" when the Government, applying "stop-go-stop" techniques, had restricted the home trade, slashed the margin of profit and made exporting hell.) But Chancellor Maudling was more circumspect than Macmillan. He was careful to say that while they could not control wages they could always take care of profits—by appropriate taxation. He leant over backwards to try to convince the trade unionists that restraint of profits was as much a Government policy as restraint of wages. But I do not suppose that the trade unionists believed him. In any case when he made that remark he knew that company profits were actually falling.

DIVISION OF THE NATIONAL INCOME—PERCENTAGES

| | *Total incomes from employment* | *Total incomes from self-employment* | *Gross profits of companies*[1] |
|---|---|---|---|
| 1938 | 62.7 | 13.4 | 14.3 |
| 1948-51 | 71.2 | 13.3 | 19.5 |
| 1952-55 | 71.6 | 11.4 | 17.7 |
| 1956-59 | 73.0 | 10.1 | 17.3 |
| 1960-62 | 74.5 | 9.7 | 16.7 |

[1] Excluding capital consumption.

(Source: Nat. Income and Expenditure Blue Books.)

It is extraordinary that Conservative leaders should have expected the trade unions to accept wage restraint while the recipients of company earnings—directors' salaries and dividends—not only remained untouched but were constantly being raised. (Dividends were, in fact, advancing faster than company earnings.) And what about profits? Were profits always to be held sacrosanct? Could profit margins never be cut when wages rose? Could managements never be expected to use

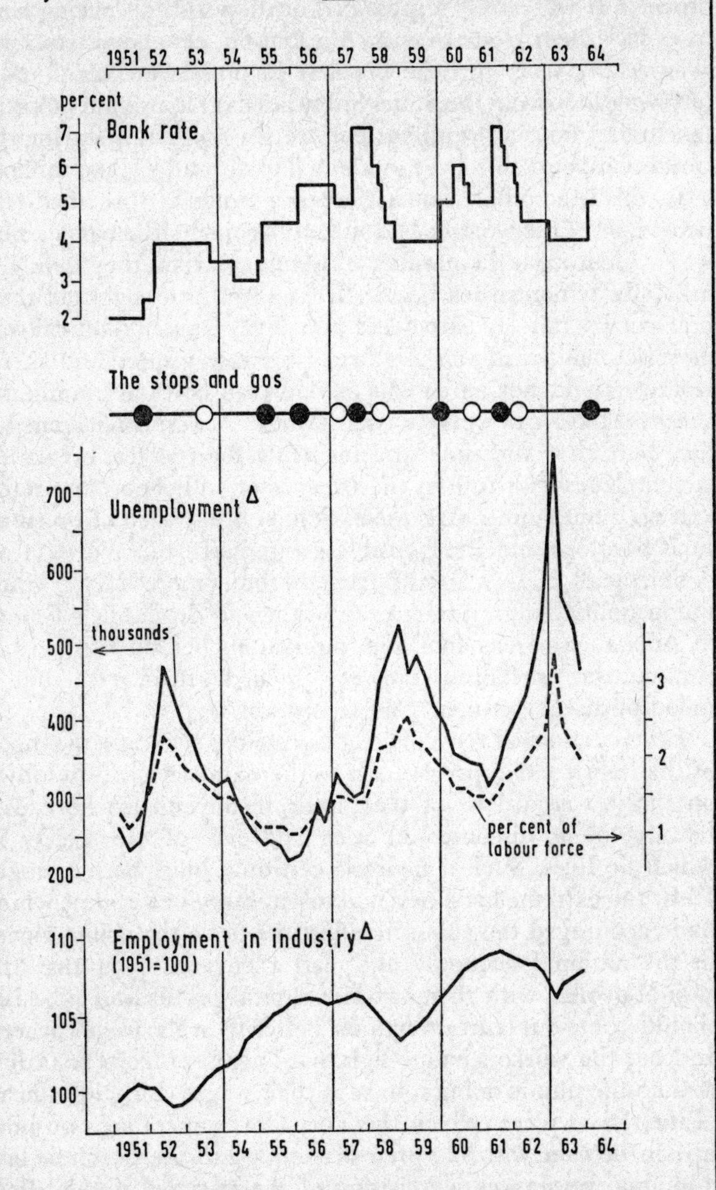

STOP-GO-STOP UNDER THE CONSERVATIVES
Key: Δ = seasonally adjusted, ● = stop (rise in bank rate), ○ = go (fall in bank rate)
1951 52 53 54 55 56 57 58 59 60 61 62 63 64
per cent
Bank rate
7
6
5
4
3
2
The stops and gos
Unemployment Δ
700
600
500
400
300
200
thousands
per cent of labour force
3
2
1
Employment in industry Δ
(1951=100)
110
105
100
1951 52 53 54 55 56 57 58 59 60 61 62 63 64

their brains to offset a rise in wages by some more intelligent organisation of their business—by better ordering of materials or by better planning of their manufacturing and distributing process? It was surely a gross provocation to the working class to expect them alone to carry the burden of income restraint—especially when private business incomes were continually receiving help from the State. Subsidies paid to private industry (excluding housing) and agriculture (in the main) during the Conservative régime have amounted to around £3,500 million.

In the Macmillan epoch the sour, cynical, "browned-off" behaviour of the workers had in fact become pathological. This was evident from the number of frivolous strikes they indulged in. Railwaymen struck because they could no longer get their hair cut by railway employees in railway time and on railway premises. Shipyard workers struck because joiners and metal workers could not agree who should drill holes in aluminium sheets. Motor-car workers even struck because managements dared to alter the time arrangements for the tea break. As Arthur Koestler wrote in the *Observer* of 10th February 1963: "In no other country has the national output been crippled on such frivolous and irresponsible grounds. In this oldest of all democracies class relations have become more bitter, trade union politics more undemocratic than in de Gaulle's France or Adenauer's Germany. The motivation behind it is neither communism, socialism, nor enlightened self-interest, but a mood of disenchantment and cussedness."

Psychiatrists will recognise these frivolous strikes as the mood of the "obstructive psychopath"—the man who will lie down on the job regardless of the public inconvenience he causes because he is discontented with and sick of the society in which he lives. Such a neurosis can only have been brought on by the extreme harshness and insensibility of a régime which had encouraged the acquisitive instinct to be the prime mover in the national economy and had then seen to it that the capital-owners with their tax-free capital profits and subsidies should come out of its growth far better than the wage earners. Indeed, the workers had to fight hard against official restraints and hostile public opinion to keep their wages rising just ahead of the rise in prices which the Tory Government kept pushing up all the time with the price of money and the purchase tax. The final result was a lowering of the national standards of behaviour and the complete estrangement of the working class.

# PART III

# INTERMISSION FOR RESEARCH

FOURTEEN

# THE EXTERNAL PROBLEM: THE BALANCE OF PAYMENTS HOAX

THE MAIN REASON why the minority ruling clique in this country has persistently pursued an economic policy which is not in the interests of the majority working mass is because of its obsession with the status of sterling, the balance of payments and the level of the gold and dollar reserves: in short, its preoccupation with the business of finance-capitalism. It has clung obstinately to the old pretence that sterling is a reserve currency which needs special protection. It is neurotically fearful that foreigners will lose confidence in it if British wages keep rising or if the shadow of a deficit begins to creep over our international trading account. It has persuaded itself—but without logic or reason—that deflation of demand is the only sure remedy which can be applied to keep wages in check and the balance of payments in equilibrium. All of this can be shown to be fanciful—the wishful thinking of the finance-capitalist's mind—but as it is a technical subject requiring statistical support I could not deal with it adequately in Part II. Hence this section is devoted to a statement in more detail of the truth about our external problem.

## Capital Movements: The Real Cause of Imbalance

How wonderful it would be if every country's exports were exactly balanced by every country's imports, so that we could all clear our transactions through a world clearing union and no country would find it necessary to hold individual reserves of gold and convertible currencies! But the world is not a brotherhood or a balanced trading organisation. Each country is trying to sell abroad as much as possible of its own produce and to buy as little as possible of other countries' produce. Self-interest is the main spring of international trade. Dog-in-the-manger could be the emblem of many a trade flag.

Economically the external problem of any country engaged in international trade is the simple one of being able to sell abroad at competitive prices sufficient goods and services to pay for all its imports of goods and services. Of course, this balancing of the international trading account is not something which has to be done each year. Provided it is balanced in the long run—and provided finance can be found for the temporary deficit—there is no reason why the world should lose confidence in the currency of a country with a temporary overdraft. Confidence would—or should—only disappear if it were thought that the country in deficit was behaving irresponsibly, that is, if it was refusing to take rational steps to balance its trading account or deal adequately with a raging domestic inflation.

The Germans have recently been pressing for a code of anti-inflationary good conduct because they have been troubled by the inflationary pressures of their neighbours. But while the advanced capitalist countries are all agreed that they should so arrange their affairs that they do not upset international equilibrium by running chronic deficits or chronic surpluses, we are not yet prepared to hand over the control of our internal monetary policy to an international code of good financial behaviour drawn up by a lot of hard-faced bankers. If we were, we might just as well return to a rigid international gold standard.

For us in the United Kingdom the external problem is more complicated because we depend more than most on international trading and because we have to import more than half our food and feeding stuffs and most of our industrial raw materials. And successive governments—Labour and Conservative—have made it worse by taking on huge military and civil obligations outside the country requiring payment in foreign currencies which have to be earned by exports. In 1938 our Government expenditure overseas was only 3% of our exports—£16 million against £533 million. In 1963 it was over 9% of our exports—£381 million against £4,274 million. What is more, the Conservative Government, being committed to the practice of finance-capitalism, which is an international system, has allowed private enterprise to invest abroad virtually as much as it pleased. The movement of capital overseas has been at the bottom of our balance of payments crises.

By investing abroad I mean only direct industrial and trading investment, not portfolio investment which is effected through the "investment dollar" pool.[1] Direct investment in the sterling

[1] Non-sterling foreign securities can be bought by British resident investors with so-called "investment dollars" obtained from the sale of

area has never required any licence: it is only investment in the non-sterling area which has needed the permission of the Bank of England. And this has been given very freely under the Conservative régime. Although a licence is still required if "official" dollars are sought, "investment dollars" can now be bought in the market at the prevailing "dollar premium" by any businessman making a foreign investment who has been refused "official" dollars. The same privilege has now been extended to those buying property abroad. Never at any time has a Conservative Government or the Bank of England stopped to consider whether investment abroad or investment at home is the more advantageous for the working population of these islands. The test has only been whether the foreign investment will produce a satisfactory profit in a reasonable time for the entrepreneur. The Conservative Government seems to have assumed that if a capital project can earn 10% it would be better to earn it abroad and send the dividend back over the exchanges in order to bolster up the £ sterling. This may well be justified if there is a state of over-full employment at home but clearly we cannot assume that a state of over-full employment is going to be perpetual and that the interests of the domestic working population need never be considered.

The Bank of England, I suspect, has been working on the assumption that the Conservative ruling clique, being finance-capitalists by training and tradition, would always want to increase British assets abroad—whether portfolio securities or direct industrial investments—in order to strengthen the creditor position of Great Britain.[1] I have often thought how happy the finance-capitalists would be if the entire industrial population were transported overseas to work in projects they had financed, leaving only a docile, non-striking force of labour to work in the service trades at home.

The amount of private long-term capital which Conservative Governments and the Bank of England allowed to be exported for investment overseas between 1952 and 1962 inclusive reached the huge total of £2,780 million. This was nearly as much as the pre-war total of our entire foreign investment accumulated over the past hundred years. As an offset foreigners

foreign securities by other British residents. When there are more buyers than sellers in this investment pool a "dollar investment" premium is established. At the moment of writing it is 10½%.

[1] See its delay in closing the "Kuwait gap", pp. 95 and 98.

invested in the U.K. in this period £1,763 million, bringing the net capital outflow to around £1,000 million.

I am not suggesting that this colossal investment overseas was unjustified on business grounds. It was concentrated in the stable developed countries of the sterling area—not in those unstable countries in most need of capital—where private capital was strongly entrenched. And it was concerned mainly with the prosperous industries—oil, mining, motors, chemicals and textiles. What I am pointing out is that this continual capital flight prevented the growth in the reserves which would normally have followed from the surpluses so painfully achieved in our current trading account. In this period—1952 to 1962—the surplus earned on "visible" and "invisible" trade was £1,024 million. But the gold reserves rose by only £343 million—and that only because of an unidentified money inflow which the official statisticians cheerfully classify as the "balancing item". Yet the inadequacy of the reserves has always been advanced as one of the main reasons why we cannot afford to take risks with the balance of payments, why the workers must not be allowed to press their wage claims and frighten the foreigners who hold some of their reserves in sterling. The payments dice have obviously been loaded against the workers: the deficits have been thrown up, as it were, in their faces in order to restrict their freedom of action to secure higher wages. On the other hand the freedom of action for capital to secure higher profits abroad has remained inviolate.

Against this point of view it may be argued that finance-capitalism has encouraged foreign capital to flow into this country for the better employment of the working population as well as private domestic capital to flow outside for the better employment of workers mainly in the sterling area. That is true. But the State does not derive so great a revenue benefit from foreign-owned capital employed in British industry as it does from home-owned capital. Nor does the individual British investor, for he is not allowed as a rule to participate in the equity of the foreign-owned enterprise in this country. The British often put up the fixed capital and the foreigner runs away with the equity profit.

Of course, there is an economic case for international finance-capitalism, that is to say, for the free movement of capital to the areas where it can most profitably be employed. But our home country is not necessarily the winner in this *laissez faire* financial system. Nor is British labour. Indeed, as labour is not allowed, or is not capable of, the same freedom of movement as capital—for the worker has a home which he may not want to uproot, while capital has no home-roots at all—it is obvious that labour and capital are not competing on the same terms. Capital has the permanent advantage.

Throughout the Conservative period there was much talk of the threat to the balance of payments from the cost-inflation induced by constantly rising wages. There were several occasions when the Tory Chancellor took severe deflationary action to check it. Yet there is no statistical evidence to support the idea that it was ever the main cause of the occasional deficit in the balance of payments. The gap or deficit on "visible" trade actually narrowed—from an annual average of £260 million in the four years 1952 to 1955 to £6 million in the four years 1956 to 1959. Leaving out the exceptional year 1960, when there was a huge import excess, the only significant deterioration in the balance of payments over the period from 1952 to 1963 is to be found in the "invisible" account. The net receipts from "invisible" items fell from £447 million a year in 1952 to £120 million in 1960-61 and to about £170 million in 1962-63. This was due partly to the decline in shipping receipts but mainly to the steady rise in Government expenditure abroad which increased from £54 million in 1952 to £381 million in 1963. In the last fifteen years we have spent about £80 million a year maintaining the necessary watch on the Rhine, which adds up to £1,200 million on this single item of defence.

The claim that deflation at home has been required to protect the balance of payments is therefore false. It was Government military spending overseas which needed deflation. It was the private transfer of capital for investment abroad which called for restraint. Yet Conservative Governments have never hesitated to blame the workers and their wage claims whenever the balance of payments dipped into the red or the gold reserves fell. A blind eye was always cast on the movement of private capital abroad.

## Exchange "Crises" under Labour

If we subject the so-called "crises" in the balance of payments since the war to detailed examination we will find that it proves my thesis—that the root of the trouble has been capital and not labour.

We need not waste time over the exchange alarms of 1947. Capital was the sole cause of this convertibility crisis. The Bank of England had advised Dalton that it was safe to implement the clause of the American loan agreement which pledged us after twelve months to make sterling freely convertible for all current as distinct from capital transactions. The outer sterling area and the non-sterling area found this opportunity too good to miss and withdrew over £150 million from London in the ten days of lunacy before the convertibility privilege was withdrawn. Dalton told me that he never forgave Cobbold, the then Deputy Governor, for this wrong advice. In his memoirs, *High Tide and After, 1945-60*, he wrote: "I am still surprised, looking back, by this profound error of practical judgment. It is quite clear now that we had no chance at all of holding this degree of convertibility in mid-1947." But he should not have been so unaware of what capital would do in a world which was desperately short of dollars. It should have been clear all along that no businessman would miss any chance of exchanging sterling for dollar deposits. I calculate that in the years 1946-47 the current trading deficit accounted for only three-fifths of the loss of gold. About £500 million represented the flight of capital out of sterling.

The Labour Government—and Dalton in particular—cannot escape blame for allowing the huge American and Canadian loans to be frittered away in one year and a half—they were exhausted by October 1947—when they were intended to last at least three years or more.[1] But Dalton was an innocent babe in the financial wood. He never understood the finance-capitalist's mind and he always expected old Etonian bankers to see things through the spectacles of an old Etonian socialist.

In the 1949 crisis when Cripps got into a panic and plunged into a too drastic devaluation of the £ there was no hint that British labour costs were above world labour costs. Trouble came from the overseas sterling area which fell into a trading deficit with the dollar area when a sharp American recession brought the prices of primary commodities tumbling down.[2] If there was any difficulty in the export trade it lay with management and not with labour. The fact that the British share

[1] See *The Management of the British Economy, 1945-60* by J. C. R. Dow, Cambridge University Press, 1964, pages 20 et seq.

[2] In the first quarter of 1949 the overseas sterling area deficit with the dollar area was £72 million and in the second quarter £149 million.

U.K. BALANCE OF PAYMENTS UNDER LABOUR IN £ MILLION

| | *1938* | *1946* | *1947* | *1948* | *1949* | *1950* | *1951* |
|---|---|---|---|---|---|---|---|
| Imports f.o.b. | 835 | 1,082 | 1,560 | 1,794 | 1,978 | 2,390 | 3,501 |
| Exports and re-exports f.o.b. | 533 | 920 | 1,146 | 1,604 | 1,847 | 2,254 | 2,752 |
| Visible balance | −302 | −162 | −414 | −190 | −131 | −136 | −749 |
| Invisibles net | +232 | −133 | −28 | +197 | +169 | +433 | +330 |
| OF WHICH | | | | | | | |
| Government net | −16 | −323 | −149 | −76 | −139 | −136 | −150 |
| Shipping net | +20 | +29 | +36 | +80 | +95 | +141 | +132 |
| Interest, profits and dividends net | +175 | +81 | +93 | +91 | +99 | +159 | +147 |
| Net current balance | −70 | −295 | −442 | +7 | +38 | +297 | −419 |
| Balance of long-term capital | | n.a. | n.a. | n.a. | n.a. | n.a. | n.a. |
| Balancing item | | n.a. | n.a. | n.a. | n.a. | n.a. | n.a. |
| Balance of monetary movements (a) (b) | | +295 | +412 | −145 | −192 | +437 | +376 |
| Gold and and currency reserves (at end of year) | | 664 | 512 | 457 | 603[1] | 1,178 | 834 |

n.a. Not available in form now used.

(a) + = fall: − = rise.

(b) Including balance of long-term capital and balancing item.

[1] After giving effect to the devaluation: there was, in fact, a loss of £3 million in the year.

in the world's exports of manufactures continued to decline after the 1949 devaluation—in spite of an 18% differential in favour of British export prices compared with American[1]—suggests that British management was not on its export toes.

Douglas Jay gave the wrong impression in his contribution to *Hugh Gaitskell, 1906 to 1963* when, boasting of the wonderful effects on trade of the Crippsian devaluation, he said: "Gold flowed in continuously from September 1949 to June 1951." Gold flowed in because the foreign capitalist had stopped his speculative selling of the £. In fact, speculation turned on the £ being written up. Gold came in because foreign capital flowed in. Finance-capitalism was really responsible for the joy in Jay's heart.

The 1951 crisis I have already discussed.[2] This again was not a labour-cost crisis. It was the enforced re-armament, the inevitable stocking-up and the adverse terms-of-trade which caused the £419 million deficit on our international account. This crisis, which defeated the Attlee administration, gave Labour a bad administrative name but the workers must surely be held free from blame.

## Exchange "Crises" Under the Conservatives

When the Conservatives re-gained power a balance of payments surplus was paraded before the public as the primary aim of their economic policy. Butler at one time suggested that a surplus of £400 million a year should be our target. This was never realised but whenever the surplus fell short of expectations the workers' wage claims were invariably held up to reproach as the stumbling block on the road to solvency. Professor Robbins in the Stamp Memorial Lecture in November 1951 had declared that balance of payments equilibrium should be regarded as the sole test of sound financial policy. "The persistence of external disequilibrium", he said, "can always be attributed to a failure of financial policy. Equilibrium can be reached only if monetary policy is restored to its rightful place." When Thorneycroft came to rule at the Treasury Robbins was generally regarded as the inspirer of his "hard money" madness.

[1] See Miss P. Ady on "Terms of Trade" in *The British Economy in the Nineteen Fifties*, Clarendon Press, Oxford, 1962.

[2] See p. 61 et seq.

After the 1951 crisis, solved by the orthodox means of import cuts designed to save £600 million, the Conservative Government had to deal with three more exchange flurries —1955, 1957 and 1960-61. In the 1955 crisis, the only occasion when the country was threatened by an excess demand type of inflation, there was much talk of unreasonable wage demands and when foreign selling of the £ broke out it was attributed to this inflationary factor. But this was really wishful thinking. The speculation against the £ was, in fact, due to other causes and in particular to a foreign misunderstanding of British exchange policy which arose out of the Paris meeting in July of the O.E.E.C. convened to consider the winding-up of the European Payments Union. Rumour had gone around that the British were considering either a devaluation of the £ or a floating £ or the widening of the permitted 1% spread in exchange dealings. The rumour was denied by Butler and finally killed at the I.M.F. meeting in Istanbul in September. But by this time the Chancellor was committed to a deflationary policy and as usual the workers, through the rise in unemployment, took the rap.

No further attacks on sterling were made until the Suez crisis in the autumn of 1956. Chancellor Macmillan was the first senior minister to "rat" on that miserable adventure and it is believed that he forced Eden to withdraw when the troops had nearly completed their mission by telling him that the £ was about to collapse as the Americans had refused to support it. Later Macmillan borrowed £200 million from the I.M.F. and secured stand-by credits of £400 million from the I.M.F. and the U.S. Export-Import Bank. Deflationary measures were, of course, added with a special tax on petrol and oil and some increase in the purchase tax schedules.

The 1957 payments crisis was the "phoniest" of the lot, with Chancellor Thorneycroft trying to put the blame on to the trade unions for their excessive wage claims. The British investor had taken alarm at the threat of domestic inflation and had been madly rushing for some time into dollar securities through the so-called "Kuwait gap".[1] This was finally plugged

[1] Until the "Kuwait" gap was closed in July 1957 U.K. residents could acquire foreign currency securities from residents of the overseas sterling area. In 1957 there was a rush on the part of British nationals to transfer funds to Kuwait and with these funds to buy transferable sterling in Beirut. This transferable sterling was then used to buy American and Canadian securities. In two and a half years the gap swallowed £160 million.

U.K. BALANCE OF PAYMENTS UNDER THE CONSERVATIVES
IN £ MILLION

| *Current acct.* *visible trade* | *1952* | *1953* | *1954* | *1955* | *1956* | *1957* | *1958* | *1959* | *1960* | *1961* | *1962* | *1963* |
|---|---|---|---|---|---|---|---|---|---|---|---|---|
| Imports f.o.b. | 3,048 | 2,927 | 2,989 | 3,386 | 3,324 | 3,538 | 3,360 | 3,617 | 4,106 | 4,013 | 4,059 | 4,318 |
| Exports and re-imports f.o.b. | 2,769 | 2,683 | 2,785 | 3,073 | 3,377 | 3,509 | 3,407 | 3,522 | 3,728 | 3,883 | 3,991 | 4,274 |
| Visible balance | −279 | −244 | −204 | −313 | +53 | −29 | +47 | −95 | −378 | −130 | −68 | −44 |
| Invisibles net | +447 | +392 | +329 | +157 | +154 | +245 | +295 | +235 | +120 | +120 | +170 | +165 |
| OF WHICH "Invisibles" | | | | | | | | | | | | |
| Government net | −54 | −58 | −126 | −139 | −172 | −147 | −224 | −233 | −287 | −336 | −367 | −381 |
| Shipping net | +134 | +88 | +36 | −30 | −48 | +7 | +43 | +5 | −38 | −31 | −19 | −19 |
| Interest, profits and dividends net | +258 | +329 | +255 | +174 | +224 | +239 | +300 | +272 | +238 | +253 | +322 | +341 |
| Net current balance | +168 | +148 | +125 | −156 | +207 | +216 | +342 | +140 | −258 | −10 | +102 | +121 |
| Balance of long term capital account | −134 | −194 | −191 | −122 | −187 | −106 | −183 | −487[1] | −187 | +44 | −89 | −147 |

| | | | | | | | | | | | | |
|---|---|---|---|---|---|---|---|---|---|---|---|---|
| OF WHICH | | | | | | | | | | | | |
| Private investment:— | | | | | | | | | | | | |
| abroad | −127 | −173 | −238 | −182 | −258 | −298 | −298 | −307 | −313 | −327 | −259 | −330 |
| in the U.K. | +13 | +28 | +75 | +122 | +139 | +126 | +165 | +176 | +228 | +416 | +275 | +288 |
| Balancing item | +61 | +29 | +49 | +122 | +43 | +97 | +43 | −58 | +255 | −14 | +86 | −129 |
| Balance of monetary movements (a) | −95 | +17 | +17 | +156 | −63 | −207 | −202 | +405 | +190 | −20 | −99 | +115 |
| Gold and currency reserves (at end of year) | 659 | 899 | 986 | 757 | 799 | 812 | 1,096 | 977 | 1154 | 1185 | 1,002 | 949 |

(a) + = fall: − = rise.

[1] Included £232 subscriptions to I.M.F., etc.

D

in July. The foreign speculation which developed against the £ in August was not due to apprehension about British labour costs but to rumours of devaluation. The French franc had been devalued in all but name[1] and it was thought by foreign speculators that at the I.M.F. meeting in September the German mark might be upvalued and the £ devalued. At the I.M.F. meeting this was duly contradicted but the speculative flurry had given Thorneycroft an excuse for raising Bank rate to 7% on 19th September and clamping down on growth in the whole economy. He actually told an audience in New York, where he had gone for the I.M.F. meeting, that he was prepared to press his deflationary measures to the point when they would create serious unemployment if the £ could be saved.

There was nothing in the "visible" or "invisible" trade items to justify a demand deflation in 1957.[2] The crisis was caused simply by the flight of nervous capital—foreign and domestic. The domestic flight of capital into portfolio investment abroad should have been stopped before it had assumed such alarming proportions. It was a shock to learn from Thorneycroft's evidence at the Bank Rate Tribunal that the Bank of England had known all along about the Kuwait leak and had been slow to stop it.

The 1960-61 exchange crisis developed out of the trading deficit of £258 million in 1960, which was due partly to a decline in "invisible" income, partly to a rise in "invisible" debits, but mainly to the sharp rise in imports. A flight of foreign capital gathered pace in the first half of 1961. This was, in effect, the return home of the "hot money" which had been attracted to London by the high Bank rate.[3] (This only goes to show how improvident it is to protect a currency by offering high rates of interest to foreign bankers.) A wage-cost inflation did not come into it. As one economist put it: "The crisis was not, in fact, occasioned by the state of the current balances, but by a massive outflow of capital. As this outflow was due to events elsewhere a policy mainly concerned with

[1] By an export subsidy of 20% and a tax of 20% on imports in August 1957.

[2] In the first half of the year an overall surplus had actually been secured on the balance of payments and the year ended with a total surplus of £216 million.

[3] Between March and December 1960 sterling balances held by foreigners rose from £822 million to £1,405 million. In the first three-quarters of 1961, over £500 million of foreign deposits were withdrawn.

deflation was hardly likely to check it".[1] But that argument was lost on Selwyn Lloyd.

It had by that time become Conservative policy to hold down domestic employment and trade below its optimum level simply to avoid the risk of imports rising too much and throwing the balance of payments into deficit. The real Conservative motive in a balance of payments surplus was to preserve the maximum freedom for finance-capitalism—especially for its investment abroad. As Scott wrote in *The British Economy in the 1950's*: "The prime objective of policy was to strengthen sterling, which may be interpreted as the maintenance of the existing exchange rate coupled . . . with a high degree of freedom for foreign capital transactions." By a stroke of luck the Conservative Chancellors were able to pursue this finance-capitalist policy without causing too much damage at home partly because there was an unusually rapid growth in the world trade in manufactures, so that our exports went on expanding, partly because the terms of trade were steadily improving. In other words, the balance was attainable without too severe a deflation—except under Selwyn Lloyd. But the fact was not lost on the trade unions that this external policy was conceived in the interests of capital and not in the interests of the working class. It was a policy which slowed down the growth of employment and the rise in living standards. Patrick Gordon Walker said in the House of Commons debate on the Thorneycroft deflation: "It is very difficult to avoid the conclusion that one of the main objects was really to declare war on the trade unions."

### THE STERLING MYSTIQUE

How did the fantastic idea come about that sterling is a sacred "reserve" currency which needs special care and protection—even at the expense of the full employment and well-being of the British working population?

"The Crown and the £ sterling", said the late Per Jacobsson, Director-General of the International Monetary Fund, "are the twin pillars of British greatness". Certainly, the higher civil servants in the Treasury and the Bank of England are expected to honour and revere the £ sterling as they do the monarchy. The two are part and parcel of the whole British mystery.

Most people now believe that the respectability of the City of

[1] A. R. Conan in *Westminster Bank Review* of November, 1963.

London is indissolubly linked with the respectability of sterling. This ridiculous notion was actually put before the Halsbury Committee on the decimalisation of the coinage[1] by the representatives of the Bank of England, the City Establishment, Sir Geoffrey Crowther and all. The £, they said, was part of the public image of the City of London and tampering with it would be damaging to the bread and butter business of the City bankers, merchants and agents which, they claimed, earned a profit of £150 million in a good year. The Bank of England went so far as to declare that this argument was *crucial*, that it was not a matter of sentiment, but of livelihood—as if the livelihood of the few hundred highly paid executives and the few thousand poorly paid clerks who work in City banking and finance could be compared with the livelihood of the many millions of people who produce the £4,000 million worth of goods for export! The representatives of the British Insurance Association even told the Halsbury Committee that "the idea of the £ sterling was intrinsically bound up in the minds of many foreigners, particularly in some middle eastern countries where a great deal of British insurance business originated, with the idea of London as solid, secure and financially trustworthy". Perhaps they were trying to convince the Arab Boycott Committee that the mystique of the £ sterling was historically a native religious cult and not derived from the Jewish faith.

The truth of the matter is that the prestige of London as a world financial centre rests not on the mystique of the £ sterling but on the practical and unique facilities which the City offers within its one square mile to any credit-worthy foreign trader who can fix up his finance, insurance, and shipping by signing little scraps of paper which are always honoured. As the minority report of the Halsbury Committee pointed out: "The City does itself less than justice by suggesting that a large section of foreign customers might take their business elsewhere . . . and so deprive themselves of the continued enjoyment of the integrity and unrivalled services and experience which the City gives." Even the Bank of England in its *Bulletin* of December 1963 admitted: "In today's conditions, when funds can and do move freely, the decisions as to whether or not to hold sterling are increasingly dependent on conditions of commercial and financial advantage."

[1] White Paper: Cmnd. 2145, 1963.

As Britain has been the world's greatest trader and as the City of London has always offered unique facilities to foreign merchants, sterling was naturally the most widely used currency in international trade before the United States emerged as the world's strongest and richest power. For convenience many foreign merchants kept their cash reserves in London and even before 1914 some foreign central banks began the practice in a small way of holding sterling balances in London. The strong desire on the part of our finance-capitalists to return to pre-1914 conditions was, as I have said, decisive in the great debate in 1925 on the return to gold at the old rate, although this meant over-valuing the £ and creating more unemployment.

When the £ was pushed off its gold pedestal in 1931 the City bankers believed that the end of their world had come but it soon became evident that our overseas trade was deriving great benefit from a cheaper £ and a fluctuating exchange. The £, however, did not float freely; it was managed. In April 1932 the Exchange Equalisation Fund had been set up to operate in the exchanges and to obviate extreme fluctuations in the sterling rate. The management was highly successful —for which the Bank of England mechanics deserve high praise —and the fund soon built up reserves of considerable size. (The gold reserves rose from £199 million at the end of June 1932 to £361 million in June 1933 and to £428 million in June 1934.) It is only fair to point out, however, that as the world depression deepened in the nineteen-thirties there was increasing distrust of the dollar and a growing confidence in sterling under the management of a "safe" National Government with a Conservative Chancellor (Chamberlain) at the Treasury.

Both before and after the First World War there had been an endless debate among the academic economists as to whether stability of the exchange rate or stability of the domestic price level was to be preferred. Those who preferred fixity argued that a floating exchange tends to fall too low during a confidence crisis and to rise too high when the crisis is over, so that countries require to have larger gold reserves than they would need under a fixed exchange system. Those who preferred a stable price level or an expanding economy at home pointed to the fact that a floating exchange takes the economic strains as they come, so that a high Bank rate—that damper of domestic trade—is no longer called for to protect the exchange value of the currency.

Keynes supported for a time a floating exchange. In his *Tract on Monetary Reform*, he had written:

> In pre-war days when almost the whole world was on a gold standard we had all plumped for stability of exchange as against stability of prices and we were ready to submit to the social consequences of a change of price level for causes quite outside our control. . . . We submitted partly because we did not dare trust ourselves to a less automatic (though more reasoned) policy and partly because the price fluctuations experienced were in fact moderate. Nevertheless, there were powerful advocates of the other choice. In particular the proposals of Professor Irving Fisher for a compensated dollar.[1]

Keynes thought that the choice between stability of the exchange or stability of the price level was not necessarily the same for all countries. The decision must depend on the relative importance of foreign trade in the economic life of the country. Nevertheless he expressed a preference for stability of prices if it could be achieved, although he doubted the wisdom of the Irving Fisher scheme for a compensated dollar. As he wanted to see cheap money put to work at home for trade expansion Keynes suggested at the Macmillan Committee in 1931 that the Treasury should use a high money rate for external purposes and a low money rate for internal purposes. Montagu Norman, the Governor of the Bank, was horrified and became speechless at the Committee's session when confronted with this unconventional idea. Like all other finance-capitalists he could only think of demand deflation as the means of correcting an adverse movement in the sterling exchange.

The experience of the managed exchange in the nineteen-thirties certainly showed up the advantages of a floating £ in a period of massive unemployment. Bank rate was brought down to 2% and there it stayed until the start of the Second World War. Cheap money was made freely available for business expansion at home. And expansion did come. Industrial investment was encouraged and a boom almost developed in housing.

It was during this period of fluctuating exchange that the

[1] These were given in the *Manchester Guardian* Reconstruction Supplement 7th December 1922. The scheme involved adjusting the value of the dollar automatically by reference to an index number of prices.

sterling area was developed as a currency bloc and the £ sterling came to gain its reputation as a "reserve" currency. Sterling was the currency in use not only for the British Commonwealth (excepting Canada) but for the Scandinavian countries, Japan, Egypt, Turkey, Portugal and the Argentine, which had all followed the £ in its divorce from gold. Over 40% of world trade was then being settled in sterling. The practice grew of central banks holding reserves in sterling and making settlements in sterling. There were even occasions when countries devalued their currencies against sterling, not against gold, as Australia did in 1930—and as Hungary had done in 1924. It might be said that there was then a possibility that the sterling system—under aggressive and skilled management—would replace the old gold standard but with the coming of the Second World War that chance disappeared for all time.

When hostilities broke out in 1939 the floating exchange came to an abrupt end. A fixed parity with the dollar at $4·03 to the £ was established and there it remained fixed for the rest of the war. The loose sterling area system became clearly defined and legalised as the "scheduled territories" of the Commonwealth (excepting Canada) Japan, Sweden, Palestine, Jordan, Iraq, Libya and Iceland. Rigid exchange controls were put into force and all the earnings of currencies other than sterling by members of the "scheduled territories" had to be surrendered to the authorities in London who managed the central dollar pool. Surplus balances accruing to the members of the pool were always convertible into dollar and other currencies according to their needs, but needs were interpreted strictly and there was no conversion in excess of them.[1] The war left, of course, huge sterling debts owing to Commonwealth and Allied countries. The amounts were £2,500 million due to the sterling countries and £1,200 million due to the non-sterling countries (against £540 million and £230 million respectively before the war). These balances gave sterling the reputation of a "reserve" currency although its use as a world currency after 1945 was not, in fact, as extensive as it was pre-1914.

[1] There was never any convertibility for private residents either in the U.K. or in the sterling area overseas except within certain narrow limits and in certain conditions laid down by the exchange control authorities (e.g. foreign travel, change of domicile, sickness and hardship, etc.).

The Americans suspected that these vast sterling deposits would give the U.K. an export advantage. Would not our creditors prefer to buy British goods when the cash lay ready in London? So in the American loan agreement we were put under an obligation to try to get them reduced. Dalton left this negotiation to a Treasury official he admired, Wilfred Eady, who frankly did not believe in its wisdom. He probably agreed with the Americans that a great pile of sterling debt held by overseas creditors would act as an inducement to buy British goods. So nothing came of these negotiations and the chance to reduce the foreign interest bill was lost. Australia and New Zealand accepted some cuts but no one else. At a later date, as these balances were regarded as a threat to sterling, being withdrawable on demand, it was suggested that they should be blocked or funded or handed over to the I.M.F. in exchange for I.M.F. deposits (the I.M.F. taking a long-term bond from the U.K.). Nothing was done—the Radcliffe Committee later on did not favour any action—and the sterling area countries have on the whole found it useful to draw on their balances when they are in deficit to the dollar area and to let them pile up when they are in surplus. This little convenience can hardly be called a "sterling system".

The war left a great mass of unconvertible sterling held by non-dollar and non-sterling accounts. In 1954 all non-sterling and non-dollar sterling accounts were unified into one "transferable account" sterling which for some time was quoted at a slight discount on official sterling. In that year the old commodity markets in London were gradually re-opened with limited arbitrage allowed on dollar commodities. Then in February 1955 the Bank of England was authorised to support the "transferable" sterling rate which gave in effect "de facto" convertibility to the holders. Finally, in December 1958 official sterling and "transferable" sterling were formally amalgamated, leaving only "security" sterling outstanding and separately quoted. This is sterling acquired by dollar and non-dollar foreigners for the purpose of making a portfolio investment in the U.K. It is quoted as I write as a discount of ¼%.

The idea that sterling is an important "reserve" currency does not survive examination. As Nicholas Kaldor and Professor Tinbergen said in the paper they submitted to the Geneva Conference on the developing nations: "To be widely acceptable as an international reserve a currency must be strong in the sense that nobody seriously contemplates its devaluation: but to make a contribution to the stock of reserves owned by other countries a currency must be weak in the sense that the country in question must have a deficit in its balance of payments." That is the paradox inherent in the reserve currency idea. Sterling can never be a key reserve currency because it is not fully convertible. The dollar is in theory the only true reserve currency because it is on paper fully convertible and because its value is fixed by weight in gold. But even the dollar is not freely convertible. The Federal Reserve have been able to restrain foreign currency authorities from freely converting their dollar balances into gold at Fort Knox.

Sterling will continue to be widely and freely used in international trade not because it is a key reserve currency but because we British are great international traders and because London offers unique banking, insurance, shipping and air facilities to the foreign merchant. What is more, foreign bankers recognise that it is a sound enough currency to use for all practical banking purposes, for the liquid assets behind it are much larger than banks usually require in their own business. In its quarterly bulletin for March 1964 the Bank of England disclosed the figures of our external assets and liabilities as at the end of 1962 classified as "short-term" and "long-term" (twelve months being the dividing line) and as "official" and "private".[1] The Bank assures us that the effect of the incompleteness or unavailability of statistics for several important

[1] U.K. EXTERNAL ASSETS AND LIABILITIES: END 1962

IN £ MILLIONS

| *Assets* | | *Liabilities* | |
|---|---|---|---|
| Short-term | | Short-term | |
| (*a*) Official (gold reserves) | £1,002 | (*a*) Official | £2,462 |
| (*b*) Private claims, sterling and non-sterling | 2,104 | (*b*) Private | 2,738 |
| Long-term | | Long-term | |
| (*a*) Official—loans, etc. | 684 | (*a*) Official | 2,640 |
| —$ shareholdings | 385 | | |
| (*b*) Private—portfolio | 3,000 | (*b*) Private—portfolio | 735 |
| direct investments | 4,950 | direct investments | 2,100 |
| U.K. subscriptions to I.M.F. | 696 | I.M.F. sterling holdings | 517 |
| | £12,821 | | £11,192 |

items is "undoubtedly to understate U.K. external assets more seriously than the corresponding external liabilities". This is very gratifying, seeing that the grand totals showed that assets exceeded liabilities by £1,629 million—the figures being £12,821 million against £11,192 million. Call it an assets surplus of about £2,000 million and we would not be far wrong. The fact that our short-term liabilities greatly exceed our short-term assets, so that to that extent we remain dependent upon foreign confidence and the goodwill of overseas financial authorities, is a reminder that we are still indulging in the old banking habit of borrowing short (including Euro-dollars) in order to lend long as well as short. But in the face of this table who can pretend that our position as a great trading and banking nation is not a strong one? To meet the short-term liabilities of £5,200 million we had gold and convertible currency reserves of £1,002 million, official holdings of marketable dollar securities £385 million and drawing rights on the I.M.F. of £876 million (£357 million automatically), making a total of £2,263 million. No commercial banker works on such a high liquidity ratio as 43½%. Only Germany could claim to have a greater degree of solvency.

The Bank of England emphasised another point of strength. We have profitable long-term investments abroad of £7,950 million (of which £3,000 million is portfolio) against foreign investments in the U.K. of £2,835 million (of which £735 million is portfolio). So behind the £ sterling lies an immense amount of invested wealth overseas.

If foreigners want to make another "bear" attack on sterling because of a temporary deficit in our international trading account let them try! They will find the new machinery which the central banks have devised in the last few years to help protect the key currencies—the currency-swaps, the Basle agreement and now the gold pool—working so efficiently that it would hardly be worth their while to make the attempt.

## The International Payments System

To talk of an international payments "system" is a misnomer. There is no "system". The Bretton Woods agreement of 1944, which established the International Monetary Fund, did not set up any new system of international exchange. Keynes' plan for an international clearing union and a super-central world bank able to create international money (which he wanted to call by the unsympathetic name of "bancor")[1] was turned down by the Americans. It was considered to be in advance of its time. The parties to the agreement merely subscribed gold and currency to an International Monetary Fund whose members undertook to stabilise their currencies and work to certain economic and financial rules to achieve stability. The Fund was given power to extend to its members only short-term credits (maximum period five years) to enable them to meet temporary deficits on their balance of payments or "bear" attacks on their currencies in the exchange markets. That was all. And the credits were strictly limited by the amount of gold and currency subscribed. The Fund, not being a bank, had no power to create additional deposits for its members.

As the Fund made no contribution to the finance of world trade or to the development of the poorer half of the world an International Bank for Reconstruction and Development (the "World Bank") was set up at the Bretton Woods conference to make loans to credit-worthy countries for sound economic enterprises of the public works type. Later the World Bank established two subsidiaries—the International Development Association to advance money on less stringent terms to developing countries and the International Finance Corporation to make loans to private enterprise in developing countries. These organisations have done a wonderful job but they have inadequate resources for their work. The International Development Association has virtually come to the end of its financial tether.

For many years after its formation the I.M.F. remained inactive and it was not until the late Per Jacobsson became Director-General that it began to extend credits actively to the U.K. and other countries who were in exchange difficulties. The objection to the I.M.F. credit system is that it compels deficit countries to seek exchange equilibrium through monetary deflation, that is, through the sacrifice of economic growth. Deflation is the orthodox banking condition for loans to debtors in trouble. One will recall that at the time of the exchange crisis in 1931 the deflationary conditions imposed by American and French bankers in return for their credits to save the £

[1] "Bancor" calls to mind old-fashioned, pompous bankers. A better name would have been "bunkor" which suggests perhaps the phoney nature of international money.

were described as a "bankers' ramp". A similar "bankers' ramp" was repeated when Thorneycroft sought aid from Per Jacobsson at the I.M.F. in 1957. A 7% Bank rate and credit squeeze were in effect one of the conditions of I.M.F. aid. This will explain why members of the I.M.F. have not been anxious to go cap in hand to the Director-General.

When the Americans fathered the birth of the I.M.F. in 1946 they made the directors of the Fund accept the gold price of $35 per ounce which had been fixed by President Roosevelt in 1934. The directors then persuaded the members of the Fund to fix and publish their exchange parities in terms of the gold dollar. They stated at the time: "We recognise that in some cases the initial par values that are established may later be found incompatible with the maintenance of balanced international payments positions at a high level of domestic activity." Stafford Cripps proved the wisdom of these cautionary words when he devalued the £ by 30½% in September 1949 (from $4.03 to $2.80), thus raising the sterling price of gold by 44% from 172/3 to 248/- an ounce. (The present London market price is around 250/-). The rest of the sterling area followed his lead and the opportunity was then taken by France, Belgium, Italy and Portugal to effect lesser devaluations of their own currencies. No further upsets occurred until the nineteen-fifties when the French franc got into trouble. General de Gaulle, with the connivance of the I.M.F., finally devalued the franc in 1958.[1] Later—in March 1961—Germany and Holland upvalued their currencies by about 5%. In that year—as in 1957—there was a sharp attack on the £ and our exchange parity was only saved by heavy borrowings from the I.M.F. and by prompt support from the central banks. In this uneasy period the feeling grew that if the £ were allowed to slip it would bring down the dollar and the whole I.M.F. paraphernalia. Hence our nuisance value!

After the gold crisis of October 1960 it became taboo in official circles to talk of raising the price of gold. There was a widespread rumour at that time that the dollar price of gold was to be raised. On the free London market the price was forced up temporarily to $40 an ounce through the persistent demand from private hoarders. An arrangement was quickly made between the British and American authorities for the Bank of England to draw gold from Fort Knox whenever the

[1] By 17½%.

private hoarding demand exceeded the supply of new gold from South Africa. This brought the market price back to normal. As the result of this success a formal gold consortium was set up a year later with the Bank of England as operating agent, the European central banks contributing one half and the U.S. Federal Reserve the other. The consortium sells when hoarders or speculators drive the price of gold above the New York fixed price of $35 (plus commission and shipping) and buys when it falls below. In 1962 it had to sell most of its stocks, for the hoarders took no less than 75% of the South African gold supply. In 1963 when Russia made large sales of gold (about $290 million), the consortium was able to regain the stock of gold which it had to sell to meet outside demands during the various crises. According to Samuel Montagu's annual bullion review the central banks will have increased their stocks of gold in 1963 by some $1,000 million.

The gold hoarders would never have been so persistent if the Americans had not involved themselves in a colossal adverse balance on their international account. In spite of the comfortable surplus of exports over imports the Washington government had run up a gigantic deficit through their heavy spending on defence overseas, through their huge foreign aid bill (including, of course, military aid) and through their persistent export of private capital for investment in foreign countries, which reached $3,300 million in 1963. This deficit had to be financed partly by the sale of gold, partly by arranging loans with the central banks. The result was that American gold stocks which had been as high as $24,500 million in the late 'forties and $22,500 million in the late 'fifties, had fallen below $16,000 million by the end of 1963.[1]

Now the Federal Reserve have to maintain by law a 25% gold cover for the American note issue. This is an archaic provision which no advanced capitalist system would dream of prescribing today. (The internal purchasing power of a currency is maintained, if at all, by governments trying to keep overall monetary demand within the limits of the overall supply of labour and resources.) The 25% gold cover removes out of the free American gold reserve no less than $12,000 million. This leaves only $3,600 million to meet the dollar deposits belonging to foreigners of no less than $18,000 million. A run

[1] The level at the end of June 1964 was $15,600 million. The first rise took place in that month.

on the dollar "bank" by the majority of these foreign depositors would quickly exhaust the free gold of the Federal Reserve and cause the authorities at Fort Knox to put up a notice outside their doors saying: "Gold sales suspended". And the dollar price of gold would then soar to perhaps $70 an ounce before tempting the gold hoarders to unload.

Of course the law governing the 25% gold cover would probably be abolished before such a crisis could occur. But when Kennedy proposed its abolition in 1961 he met with such a stiff resistance that the idea was postponed indefinitely.

The dollar has been saved partly because McNamara, the Secretary of Defence, has been very successful in cutting down the defence payments overseas, partly because Congress has found it easier under President Johnson to slash the Foreign Aid bill, partly because Roosa of the Treasury has been clever enough to make "swap" arrangements with foreign central banks, virtually getting them to agree that dollar convertibility into gold at Fort Knox must not be pressed. The dollar crisis seemed to have passed when the Treasury stated that in the first quarter of 1964 the payments deficit had dropped to an annual rate of about $1,250 million. Indeed Secretary of the Treasury Dillon in May 1964 claimed that if temporary short term capital outflows were excluded, the U.S. international account was "approximately in balance".

Meanwhile the vast amount of dollar deposits which have accrued in the hands of foreigners as a result of this prolific American spending on defence and aid overseas has been made use of by bankers for the finance of both international and internal trade. The holders of these dollars have re-deposited them with American banks in London and on the Continent which have been able to re-lend them (at higher rates) to merchant banks, international traders and even domestic manufacturers. This is known as the "Euro-dollar" system and the amount of these dollar deposits which have been put to work in this useful way is variously estimated at around $5,000 million.[1]

[1] See Dr. Paul Einzig, *The Euro-dollar System*, Macmillan, 1964. A "Euro-dollar" transaction simply means that a dollar deposit is transferred from one deposit account with an American bank to another deposit with an American bank, either in London or on the Continent. The American banking system as a whole continues to be responsible for the deposit. It means that international liquidity has been enhanced through the increase in the velocity of circulation of these dollar deposits.

All this had technically improved international liquidity but not necessarily international trade. The "Euro-dollar" facilities have sometimes been used by "bears" of the dollar for speculative forward buying of gold (without covering the forward exchange), so that the pressure on the spot dollar has been increased. But the main objection to the Euro-dollar "system" is that with America steadily reducing its overseas deficit the supply of dollars cannot be increased: indeed, relative to world trade, it can only be reduced.

It is extraordinary that in this age of great scientific discovery the western world has been unable to invent a new international currency or payments system. How could we run our domestic trade if businessmen were unable to borrow from banks for stock-in-trade or their short-term capital commitments? How could we expand our domestic economy if we did not have the means of increasing our money supply *pari passu* with the increase in output? In international trade there is no world central bank to borrow from, there is no institution which can extend credits to needy countries for the purchase of the raw materials and manufactures essential for the development of their trade. It seems incredible that countries cannot increase their imports for ordinary stocking-up unless they themselves have adequate reserves of gold and convertible currencies or are able to obtain long-term credits from the exporting countries.

Leaving aside the surplus dollar deposits of foreign bankers which can be used in the "Euro-dollar" market, the total amount of the national reserves of gold and convertible currencies held by the rich industrial countries is in fact the total amount of "liquidity" for the finance of international trade. This volume of liquidity has not been increased proportionately to the increase in international trade for the simple reasons, first, that the increase in the supply of new gold has not kept pace with the increase in the world output of goods, and, secondly, that the gold holding countries have never yet agreed to write-up the price of gold to match the rise in the prices of commodities. This is really a very odd situation. The gold holding countries have preferred to go on down-grading or devaluing gold—making its monetary price completely unrealistic in terms of purchasing power over commodities—rather than give a bonus to the big gold-producing countries—South Africa and Russia. The Americans do not wish to strengthen the economic power of Russia. The western democracies do not wish to strengthen the economic power of South Africa, which is pursuing an apartheid policy repugnant to the liberal world. The point has now been reached where to achieve the purpose of bringing international "liquidity" into line with the present value of international trade the price of gold would have to be at least doubled or probably trebled. Certainly that would give too large an uncovenanted profit to the gold holders and producers, not to mention the gold hoarders. No one wants a gold boom while half the world is starving. Besides, doubling the price of gold would not help the poorer nations who have none: and it would do nothing to improve the existing maldistribution of the world's gold stocks. It would merely increase the world cost of maintaining the status of gold as an international currency.

Some forward-looking politicians (like the late President Kennedy) are convinced that gold should not be brought back into greater use as a medium of international exchange. The world has been able to get along with smaller quantities of gold (none for most domestic currencies) and in the end may be able to dispense with gold altogether except for the reserves which an individual nation may feel it necessary to keep in the event of war. But even this idea may change. In the last war Great Britain managed to survive without having an ounce of gold at the Bank of England. This was simply because its great ally, America, was able to supply it with the goods it required and extend unlimited credits.

### Reconstruction of the I.M.F.

The late President Kennedy in his message to Congress in July 1963 on the measures he proposed to take for the protection of the dollar, admitted that the notional international payments "system" needed strengthening, that the U.S. has an interest "in the continuing evolution of the system inaugurated at Bretton Woods", and that adequate provisions should be made "for the growth of international liquidity to finance expanding world trade". Several plans have been put forward for the reform of the I.M.F. and its conversion into a deposit-creating central bank.

First, Professor Triffin of Yale proposed to convert the I.M.F. holding of dollars and sterling into a new international currency (backed by corresponding long-term claims against the U.S.A. and the U.K.) and to reinforce this currency by compulsory purchases of part of the gold reserves now held independently by member countries.

Next, Bernstein has suggested (i) that members' present quotas at the I.M.F. should be integrated with their working gold and currency reserves, so that these should at least appear bigger (which seems a sensible idea); (ii) that the I.M.F. should be allowed to draw on the surplus countries' reserves against the issue of its own notes and re-lend these reserves to other member countries who might be in need. He was anxious to get what he called "reverse stand-by" agreements to support either of the two key currencies, the £ and the dollar, if they were to come under pressure. This is a plan which the late Per Jacobsson favoured as it was within the competence of the I.M.F. Articles of Association.

Another suggestion half-way between the Triffin and Bernstein schemes was proposed by Maudling at the I.M.F. meeting in 1962. All these plans have been considered by two official working parties set up at the I.M.F. meeting —one in Paris on behalf of the European gold powers,[1] and the other committee in Washington on behalf of the I.M.F. But no drastic scheme of reform of the monetary system has been put forward. Conventional bankers and monetary officials are poles apart in their thinking from radical American and British professors.

The objection to all these plans is that they involve the delegation of great monetary power to a supra-national institution, which at the present juncture would be politically inacceptable. Would the conservative French bankers like to see a new Director-General, who might be a Brazilian, extending huge credits to a developing African state which is crazy on spending and allergic to saving? The difficulty would be to secure really neutral management for such a reinforced and powerful I.M.F. As Khruschev has said: "No man is neutral". This is particularly true of bankers.

Kaldor of King's College, Cambridge, and Professor Tinbergen of Rotterdam, having dismissed the Triffin and Bernstein plans as politically impossible, have proposed that the I.M.F. should establish its own currency (like Keynes' bancor) which, after an initial build-up period, should be made convertible into gold and/or a bundle of commodities. The bundle would

[1] The so-called "Paris Club" who had committed themselves to make $6,000 million of credits available to the I.M.F. in case of need.

consist of thirty or more of the principal commodities in world trade which have a high degree of standardisation and a reasonable durability in storage. This new currency would be fully covered by gold and commodities except for a fiduciary issue of a fixed amount. It would be held only by the central banks of member countries of the I.M.F. which would undertake to accept it in settlement of claims in the same manner as they accept gold. The Professors' idea is that the I.M.F. should make an issue equivalent to $30,000 million, of which $5,000 million would be issued in exchange for gold, $20,000 million in exchange for commodities and $5,000 million (the fiduciary issue) against loan obligations of member countries. During the build-up period the I.M.F. would purchase commodities either in the open market or out of stocks held by the member governments at or below "declared values". The "declared value" would be the highest six-monthly average price within the two years preceding the scheme. This is an excellent but revolutionary proposal and it has no chance of being accepted in the near future. Nevertheless I am convinced that sooner or later a scheme along these lines is bound to be considered. Gold as a medium of international exchange is having its wings clipped. A combination of gold and commodities on the Kaldor lines is a logical development.[1]

In the meantime I think we should all press for the scheme put up some years ago by the United Nations Association of Charles Street, London, in the interests of the poor, undeveloped nations. It makes good commercial sense. This was to empower the I.M.F. to print "gold notes" to be used exclusively through the agency of the International Development Association for the finance of public works—what is called "industrial infra-structure investment" in the experts' jargon—in the under-developed countries. The I.D.A. would use these notes to make "soft" loans to these poor nations to enable them to buy manufactures and technical equipment and services from the industrialised nations which in turn would accept from the I.D.A. the I.M.F. notes in payment, treating them

[1] This proposal has nothing to do with L. St. Clare Grondona's plan for a British Price Stabilising Corporation set up to buy international commodities having the qualities of durability and convertibility. This is a scheme for stabilising the prices of commodities which underly the economic structure of the western world but it is clear that if a British P.S.C. were established it would help Kaldor's idea of the gold-and-commodity base for a new international currency.

as gold and adding them to their own gold reserves. It was a scheme very similar to one proposed by the economist Maxwell Stamp and it has been endorsed by Harold Wilson and the Labour party. It is the most sensible of all the I.M.F. reforms proposed and it avoids the political objection to the delegation of monetary power to a supra-national institution. The I.D.A. is a subsidiary of the World Bank and everyone has confidence in its technical efficiency and absolute integrity. It is not likely to recommend the finance of public works which are not economically viable. Moreover, the scheme would help to solve the basic economic problem of the industrialised West. How are we to keep the vast industrial machine we have created turning over and our millions of workers employed if we do not make it easy for the poorer half of the world to buy our surpluses? We are going to run into trouble if we do not soon solve this problem.

While we wait for the establishment of a deposit-creating world central bank let us not pretend that the £ sterling has to take the strain of the world's need for an international currency. Of course we must endeavour to balance our international account, but we should not halt our domestic expansion for the sake of holding the exchange rate at $2.80. If the £ sterling were to get into serious trouble we would have to consider devaluation but long before that stage is reached we could call on plenty of support, for no one wants to see the make-shift system devised at Bretton Woods break down before a better system is ready to take its place. The £ has, in other words, a nuisance value, which we should not hesitate to exploit.

One final word. If a deposit-creating world central bank on the Stamp or Kaldor lines is not created very soon to replace the so-called "reserve" currency system the western monetary world will probably split. The Brookings Institute suggested in its weighty report to Kennedy on the protection of the dollar that we might have two currency blocs—a dollar-sterling bloc comprising the U.S., the U.K. and the countries economically aligned to them (e.g. Latin America, the sterling area group, Scandinavia, the Middle East, India and much of Asia) and the European "Common Market" bloc and the countries associated with them and the French Union. The Institute envisaged fixed rates of exchange within each bloc, but recommended flexible or floating rates of exchange between the two blocs themselves which would provide a means by which any basic imbalance between the two could be corrected. This would allow the U.S. and the U.K. to pursue their national growth objectives without balance of payments constraints: it would eliminate the deflationary bias inherent in the present Bretton Woods system of fixed exchange rates. The rigidities of this system have been allowed to persist far too long. I agree with Alan Day in *The Westminster Bank Review* of August 1964 that balance of payments troubles can often be cured much more smoothly by intelligent changes in exchange rates than by tedious policies of deflation in deficit countries or of inflation in surplus countries. Few surplus countries will ever allow the inflation.

The linking-up of the dollar and the £ in one currency bloc would, if it comes about, enable one of my dreams to be realised —the decimalisation of our currency and the creation of a U.K. dollar. An American economist, Sidney Rolfe, late of Princeton, proposed this plan in an article in *The Statist* at the end of last year and I gave him what support I could in *The Spectator* (3rd January 1964). We would keep the £ as the heavy unit of account for all international settlements and we would have for internal use a British dollar currently valued at what the American dollar is worth today, namely 7/2, divided as usual into one hundred cents. We would drop our existing very inconvenient coins: they would have no associability with the cents of the new dollar. We could then all do our shopping and our household accounts in intelligible sums. Externally the foreigners would be delighted. The £, being a heavier international unit than the American dollar, would be more popular than ever as the most useful currency to employ in international trade. And external confidence in the new domestic British dollar would be strengthened because before long every foreigner would be saying: "I told you so: the American and British currencies stand or fall together. They are indissolubly linked." That is exactly what Sir George Bolton, a director of the Bank of England and Chairman of the Bank of London and South America, the greatest expert we have on foreign exchange, has been preaching for months and years.

If you tell me that I am asking the £ to escape from its troubles by riding pick-a-back on the dollar, I would reply that any escape into reality from the restraint imposed on our growth by the Conservative dream of sterling as an independent "key reserve currency" would be the greatest blessing of our time.

FIFTEEN

# THE INTERNAL PROBLEM: THE INCOMES POLICY MYTH

THE INTERNAL ECONOMIC problem is as easily stated as the external but more difficult to solve. Briefly, it is to secure the maximum growth of the economy without too much inflation, in other words, to reach the full employment of our available labour and resources without inducing too large a rise in prices. We have never yet solved this problem. Nor are we likely to before we have healed the split in our society. But note that I do not pose the problem as one of achieving full employment with no rise in prices. I believe in being realistic and attacking the possible, not the impossible. As long as the two halves of the nation are opposed to one another there is clearly no hope of achieving a stable price level. The workers will go on demanding more and more as a protest against a society which they think is managed in the interests of finance-capitalism and against the interest of the working class, and, while the wage-price spiral spins away, the State will have to come more and more to the aid of the widows, the pensioners and the rest of the poor minority on fixed incomes who are the victims of the creeping inflation.

## HARD-FACED ECONOMISTS

I have no patience with the hard-faced economists who protest that price stability is easily achieved if we are prepared to be tough with labour and run the economy with an unemployment ratio of 5% (Professor Plant) or with 2% unemployment and a 5% under-capacity (Professor Paish). According to their argument this would make it difficult, if not impossible, for the unions to go on demanding a rise in wages every year. A relatively high unemployment ratio of 5% overall would mean perhaps a 10% unemployment ratio in the so-called "development" areas and this, they add, would literally force men to move to the areas where work was being offered. Thus, we would secure in their view what we have always lacked—the mobility, if not the docility, of British labour.

These Professors are not thinking deeply enough about the problem. In a humane democratic society it is impossible to take a mechanistic view of economic forces. They ought to know that economics and sociology cannot be divorced. The social conscience today will not allow any section of the population to suffer the misery of unemployment because of the accident of its birthplace or the onset of automation in its factories. As I have said, the workers need a new charter of industrial rights which will give them compensation for redundancy, re-training in a new job and transport to, and re-housing in, the new area of employment. The mobility of labour is a highly desirable object of economic policy but the industrial worker should not be financially worse off for trying to achieve it. Economically as well as socially this mechanistic "full unemployment" policy would be disastrous, for it would involve a huge waste of resources that we could not afford. America may be rich enough to carry a 5% unemployment ratio but not Great Britain. The organisers of television and radio talks do the public a disservice in allowing this academic nonsense to be propagated.

These economists unfortunately have had a great influence upon Conservative Chancellors of the Exchequer. Thorneycroft listened to a part of Robbins (the "hard money" man) without understanding the whole. Selwyn Lloyd listened to the whole of Paish (the full unemployment man) without understanding a part. But Macmillan really began the rot in 1956 when he took the Spartan view—in spite of his Keynesian upbringing—that he had to deflate the whole economy in order to deflate an over-extended part, in short, to pull down total demand in order to restrain a wage rise in one or two industries. Robert Hall, the official economic adviser of the time, did his best to counter all this nonsense—I have described him as the best economic adviser the Treasury never listened to[1]—but he was incapable of preventing the Conservative Chancellors from pursuing an internal economic policy which, like the external policy, was bound to split our already divided society.

## A Conservative Wages Policy

Conservative economic policy was based on the erroneous theory that a wage-cost inflation was the cause of all our evils

[1] *The Spectator*, 10th September, 1963. When Sir Robert Hall resigned he wrote various articles in bank reviews revealing his disagreement with Government policy. See *Lloyds Bank Review*, January, 1963 and *Three Banks Review*, March, 1964.

—our price instability, our export shortcomings, our balance of payments deficits. Full employment, it was argued, was bound to lead to an inflationary rise in wages and as wages were the biggest factor in production costs it was essential to direct monetary and fiscal policy to the restraint of wage demands. The Conservatives appeared to be quite oblivious of the fact that management inefficiency—the lack of technical and scientific brains at the board room table—was primarily responsible for the rise in our industrial costs.

Any policy of income restriction is bound in itself to divide society into those who are poor enough to be hurt by it and those who are rich enough not to care, but a policy of wage restriction designed to deflate the worker but not the employer naturally gave the trade unions the impression that a Conservative Government was taking sides against the workers and in favour of the employers. What other conclusion could they draw when a National Incomes Commission was set up by Selwyn Lloyd to restrain the rise in wages but not the rise in prices?

An unbiased neutral Government would have told the employers that as it was their duty to offset a rise in wages by greater efficiency and by the use of more labour-saving techniques they would have to justify a rise in prices by appearing before a National Prices Commission which would have the power to order a postponement of the rise if it was considered unreasonable. Of course, a National Prices Commission would be as unworkable as a National Incomes Commission, for employers would be able to reduce quality if they were ordered to reduce prices, just as the workers would be able to secure more overtime pay if they were denied a rise in wage rates. But to have one Commission frowning upon one side and not another Commission frowning upon the other side showed a bias which was indefensible. It never seemed to occur to the Tory Government that if the working class were singled out as the naughty children in the national school of economics they might develop a neurosis and behave like the delinquent teenagers who smash up holiday resorts.

## The Types of Inflation

Some economists have distinguished between two types of inflation which they call colloquially "demand-pull" and "cost-push". A "demand-pull" inflation is built up when the aggregate monetary demand for goods and services at current prices is an excess of what the available supply of labour and resources can produce. This inflation could in theory be met by lengthening the delivery dates of the goods in demand but in practice it is usually met by a rise in prices sufficient to absorb the excess monetary pressure.

A "cost-push" inflation is created when wages rise ahead of the productivity of labour and consequently push up costs. This type of inflation could be met without raising prices if companies were willing to accept a decline in profit margins and profits or if managements succeed in cutting overheads or reducing other costs of operation, as they should do if they were efficient. But in periods of full employment it is usually met by a rise in prices, the higher costs being pushed on to the consumer without any difficulty.

It is not always easy to distinguish between the two types of inflation in their early stages—indeed the distinction is not now insisted upon so precisely—but Conservative Chancellors have often confused the two and misread the inflation indices. Thorneycroft, for example, in 1957 and Selwyn Lloyd in 1961 decided to apply a sharp monetary deflation to an economy which at the time was not suffering from any inflation—either "demand-pull" or "cost-push".

The only occasion when there might have been a "demand-pull" inflation was in 1955, but some economists would deny even this and go back to the immediate post-war years of shortages as the only period when "demand-pull" exercised a strong inflationary influence.

The first two Reports of the Council on Prices, Productivity and Incomes (published in February and August 1958), which were drafted by Dennis Robertson, virtually disclaimed the existence of a "cost-push" inflation. It was assumed that all inflation was demand inflation and was caused by workers being paid too much in wages and creating an excess demand for goods. This expressed the general feeling of the Treasury at the time and led to the belief—dear to the heart of Tory Chancellors—that the only way to deal with inflation of any sort was to damp down demand and increase unemployment. In fact, the tough Tory view was that it was necessary to "knock the hell out" of overall demand in order to suppress inflationary wage claims. "We believe", said this Council in its first report (page 71) "that the decline in the intensity of demand will tend to moderate the insistence with which wage claims are pressed." That might be true for a short period but it never lasted, as the two Oxford economists have proved who have done most of the research into the wages problem.[1]

A change of view occurred on the Council on Prices, Productivity and Incomes when Professor Phelps-Brown replaced Professor Robertson. In the fourth report (published at the end of July 1961) with Lord Heyworth in the chair instead of Lord Cohen, the Council came round to the idea that our besetting sin was a "cost-push" inflation but frankly admitted that no one section of the community could be blamed for it. The course of events in a market economy, it said, depended on all the decisions that were being taken every hour of the day at home and at work, in Government and industry, in shops and offices, in board rooms and at the negotiating table. But it was not afraid to state that when a "cost-push" inflation threatened it did not favour Government action deliberately designed—through demand deflation—to throw men and machines out of work. That sort of remedy, it remarked, "was worse than the disease". And it scorned Selwyn Lloyd's deflationary budget of April 1961 which, with its new 10% "regulator", gave the economy a push in just the opposite direction to the one needed at the time. The key-note of the report was a plea for a more sensible wages policy.

[1] See pages 133, et seq. Of course, Professor Robertson would not have agreed with the conclusions of the Oxford school. In the *Marshall Lectures* for 1960 (Cambridge University Press, p. 46) he said: "In *The Spectator* of 4th December, 1959, Mr. Davenport, one of the most sharp-tongued and contemptuous critics of the Thorneycroft policies and of the Cohen Council as originally composed, wrote these words: 'Mr. Heathcoat-Amory . . . assumed office at the Treasury after the dangerous shock treatment had been given and the patient had come round. To everyone's surprise the mental condition of the T.U.C. had been improved by the shock and thereafter excessive wage claims were either not pushed or were successfully resisted, as in the case of the London busmen.' I could not help sending Mr. Davenport a brief note, saying: 'Not to everyone's surprise; not to that of the much abused Cohen Council: see paras. 136-7 of their First Report.' I neither asked for nor received a reply to my note, nor did Mr. Davenport, as far as I know, take any occasion to qualify that 'everyone'."

I am sorry that I hurt the Professor's feelings but I am sure that if he were alive he would have changed his mind. The wage quiescence after the busmen's failure did not last long.

## A Wages Policy from O.E.E.C.

A wages policy had been the theme of many White Papers of both Labour and Conservative Governments[1] but no Chancellor had dared to put one rigidly into practice until Selwyn Lloyd bluntly proclaimed his pay pause in July 1961. The curious thing was that this wages freeze coincided with the publication by the O.E.E.C. of an excellent study on the problem of rising prices which contained the first wages policy ever agreed to by international economists of different schools of thought. It was completely ignored by Selwyn Lloyd. The eminent economists who produced the O.E.E.C. report were Fellner of Yale, Hansen of Stockholm, Kahn of Cambridge, Lutz of Zurich, de Wolff of The Hague and Gilbert, director of economics at the O.E.E.C.

Except for a few qualifying paragraphs from a minority this O.E.E.C. report unanimously recommended that European governments should have a "wages policy" to deal with the problem of a "cost-push" inflation just as they had monetary and fiscal policies to deal with a "demand-pull" inflation. The authors were all agreed on the importance of "cost-push" as an independent factor in an inflationary rise of prices, although their researches showed that there was no mechanistic relation between the demand for labour and the rate of increase in wages. Wages rose, they said, because of wage negotiations and these negotiations succeeded irrespective of whether there was a shortage of labour or not or whether there was high or low unemployment. The plain truth was that wages went on rising —not necessarily uniformly or at regular intervals—because organised labour knew how to negotiate the rises and the disorganised employers did not know how to deny them.

This was a refreshingly realistic view which this committee of experts arrived at only after a careful study of the course of wage negotiations in the different European countries. They believed that during the post-war reconstruction and the Korean war boom, organised labour had become accustomed to the idea of large increases in money wages and that with the return to more normal conditions they had continued to expect such increases, especially in the U.S.A. and the U.K., despite the fact that the gain in money income was quickly offset by

[1] See the *Statement of Personal Incomes, Costs and Prices*, Cmnd., 7321 of 1948 and *The Economic Implications of Full Employment*, Cmnd., 9725 of 1956.

higher prices. This acquired habit was motivated, they thought, by a conscious or unconscious desire to increase the share of the national income going to labour. This was certainly true of labour intentions in the U.K., but the unions were always being frustrated by the fact that in periods of full employment and high demand prices had quickly followed wages, so that the profit margins of the employers had been restored and "real" wages had lost their rise.

The wages policy which this O.E.E.C. committee of experts advocated was that governments should first of all announce that inflation of the "cost-push" type could only be avoided if the average rate of money wage increases stayed approximately within the limits corresponding to the average increase in output per man-hour. They should then publish official estimates of the increase in productivity to be expected several years ahead. This done they should inform arbitrators of these estimates and arrange to be officially represented at important wage negotiations, so that this wages policy could be properly presented. Finally, as the largest employer of labour, governments should rigidly pursue the wages policy it had set for the nation.

These proposals might have alarmed some trade unionists but it was good to see this committee utterly reject the idea that a wages problem brought about by a "cost-push" inflation could be solved by trying to deflate total demand through harsh monetary measures so as to reduce the bargaining strength of labour. Of course, when the inflation happens to be a "demand-pull" inflation they agreed that monetary and fiscal measures of deflation would be required.

The O.E.E.C. Committee added that none of the following practices so familiar to us in the U.K. could be regarded as a "wages policy"—vague exhortations to labour to exercise restraint, informal understandings for wage restraint for a period and the use of the arbitration machinery where the arbitrators are not instructed as to the average wage increase appropriate to the economy as a whole.

In its fourth report (August 1961) the Council on Prices, Productivity and Incomes had virtually adopted this O.E.E.C. report as its own policy. It recommended the Government to give an official projection for a period ahead of the extent to which productivity in the national aggregate could be expected to advance. This projection would cover the production of goods and services of all kinds (not the industrial section alone) and would be related (*a*) to the planned investment programme and (*b*) to forward assessments of manpower needs and resources. It would be an indicator of the anticipated rate of growth of the whole economy; it would be a guide for those responsible in their particular fields for the planning of production, the fixing of prices and profit margins and the settlement of wages and salaries. In other words, the projection would indicate the limits within which movements of pay and profits must lie if these were to be compatible with stable prices. It would not prescribe an absolute limit. Some industries might go beyond the limit but what their excesses meant for others would be made apparent to the public. Enlightened publicity, the Council said, was the key to success of such a wages policy.

This was the most constructive report ever made by the Council on Prices, Productivity and Incomes and it should not be held against them that such a wages policy would be quite impossible to administer in a free economy and a split society. But as the trade unions had boycotted the Council from the beginning its reports were now only of academic interest.

### The Lloydian "Incomes Policy"

Selwyn Lloyd had made up his mind that the boycotted Council on Prices, Productivity and Incomes would have to go and be supplanted by a new organisation—the National Incomes Commission—to deal with wages and by a planning body—the National Economic Development Council—to deal with investment. He hoped that the trade unions and employers would be represented on both but the trade unions rejected the N.I.C. from the start. This was not surprising seeing that the "pay pause", which he had announced in July, had run counter to all their ideas of what was legal, equitable and constitutional in wage negotiation. From July 1961 all wage awards made by the Wages Councils were actually held in suspense until the Chancellor vouchsafed to give the word for their implementation. This was not done until 31st March 1962. In the private sector arbitration went ahead without Government interference and the wage rate index actually increased by 2·4% in this period (July 1961 to March 1962), which was more than in the same periods of some later years.

In February 1962 a White Paper entitled *Incomes Policy: The Next Step* (Cmnd., 1626) was issued in which the Chancellor emphasised that it would be a negation of policy to bring the first phase, the "pay pause", to an end and to put nothing in its place. Accordingly on 10th January he had invited the Trades Union Congress to collaborate with the Government and with representatives of the employers' organisations in working out "suitable arrangements for maintaining a restraining influence on the levels of incomes during the next phase pending the evolution of a long-term incomes policy". The T.U.C., while recognising in their reply that it was a condition of reasonable price stability that increases in incomes should keep in step with the growth of production, felt unable to accept this invitation. In these circumstances, the White Paper continued:

> The Government are now issuing this statement of the principles which, in their view, should govern decisions during the next phase about the scale of increases in incomes.... The objective must be to keep the rate of increase of incomes within the long-term rate of growth of national production.

So the "guiding light" was lit. The White Paper went on:

> In recent years national production per head has risen by about 2% to 2½% a year. We ought to be able to do much better than this but on present trends it seems likely to increase at about this rate in 1962. It is accordingly necessary that the increase of wages and salaries, as of other incomes, should be kept within this figure during the next phase.

Selwyn Lloyd did not stay to carry out this manœuvre. He was summarily sacked by Macmillan and his "guiding light" of 2½% was quickly changed by Maudling to the more reasonable figure of 3½% in spite of the special pleading of the Treasury's new Economic Adviser (Professor Cairncross) who argued for 2½% before the N.I.C. in the Scottish builders' case.

Selwyn Lloyd's White Paper was primarily concerned with wages and salaries but the same principles, it said, applied to other incomes. "Continued restraint in profits and dividends is a necessary corollary of the incomes policy." The Prime Minister followed this up by a statement in the House of Commons in July 1962:

> The Government will by fiscal or any other appropriate means restrain any undue growth in aggregate profits which might follow from restraint in wages and salaries.

The second report of the National Incomes Commission (dated July 1963) went even further:

> The fundamental principle of an incomes policy has to be applied to all profits arising from the production of goods and services irrespective of whether they are subsequently retained in a business or distributed to its shareholders and bond holders. . . . In the context of an incomes policy the notion that it is the right of every industry to appropriate for itself the whole of the fruits of its own greater productivity is mistaken and should be abandoned.

Maudling welcomed "the clear and comprehensive" way in which the National Incomes Commission had dealt with the incomes question. His was the only voice heard in praise of that extraordinarily muddled statement.

### The Incomes Policy Myth

A close examination will reveal that the whole incomes policy is a myth. I do not mean that it is impossible to have a policy of restraint in regard to salaries, wages, rents, profits and dividends if the parties concerned voluntarily decide to restrain their natural instincts: I mean that it is impracticable to work out a formula of restraint which could be administratively applied to these widely different sources of income. To propagate an incomes policy which is administratively indefinable is to propagate a myth.

An incomes policy, if it means anything, implies (*a*) that in real terms the national income as a whole should not rise over a period at a greater rate than the national output as a whole and (*b*) that salaries and wages should not rise at a greater rate than the productivity of labour. (*b*) is relevant to the "policy" only if salaries and wages are pushing the national income as a whole above the limit set under (*a*). But it will not be possible to ascertain statistically whether the limit has been exceeded in any one year until at least three or four months after the close. As for the productivity of labour, it is virtually impossible to obtain a national or even an industrial figure which is reliable. It is impossible to separate, for example, the effects of changes in the quality or quantity of capital equipment. Nor can we measure the productivity of labour employed in a large number of service industries. What is the productivity of a bus driver or a power station worker or a gas or water engineer? We have to be content with a single productivity figure obtained by dividing the total gross national product by the total numbers employed. It is not very significant. It is certainly not a reliable guide for an incomes "policy". What the Government is asking people to accept as a guiding light for their various incomes is a flickering of guesses.

An "incomes policy" also assumes that Labour's share in the national income should remain constant. But the trade unions have never accepted this point or disclosed whether they are aiming at increasing their share gross or net of taxation. As I showed on page 68 the wages share (excluding employers' contribution to national insurance) of the national income has remained constant since the war at around 42%.

DIVISION OF THE NATIONAL INCOME

| | *Incomes from Employment Salaries & Wages*[1] | *Rents* | *Profits, interest etc.* |
|---|---|---|---|
| 1920-29 | 59·7% | 6·6% | 33·7% |
| 1930-39 | 62·0% | 8·7% | 29·3% |
| 1948-51 | 71·2% | 4·1% | 24·7% |
| 1952-55 | 71·6% | 4·4% | 24·0% |
| 1956-59 | 73·0% | 5·0% | 22·0% |
| 1960-62 | 74·6% | 5·5% | 19·9% |

[1] Including employers' contribution to N.H.I. and Forces' pay.

## Rents and Profits

Rents are one of the only two items in the national income which could be legislatively "controlled" in an incomes policy. (The other is dividends.) But, since the decontrol of rents by the Conservative Government, rent is the only item which is left out of the Conservative incomes policy. It is not a large item, being a little over 5½% of the national incomes, but between 1951 and 1962 it had increased by 144%—from £237 million to £579 million.

Profits on the other hand are an item which cannot be controlled at all—either by the Government which taxes them or by the companies or entrepreneurs who make them—unless wages and prices are simultaneously controlled. Profits are merely the residual surplus (if any) which is left over when all expenses, interest and depreciation have been deducted from all revenues received and stock appreciation. They are sometimes a minus figure and sometimes a grossly inflated figure. They are always going up or down, The amount will vary with the state of trade, the skill of the management and a lot of luck. Business, as Keynes once said to me, is a bet.

In January 1964—towards the end of the last Tory Parliament—a crude attempt was made by the Treasury to bring profits into the incomes "policy" in a massive document of guidance which was submitted to the National Incomes Commission in January 1964. The author of the document seems to have derived his knowledge of the business world by reading Government White Papers and statistical Blue Books, which is probably all the experience he has ever had of the workings of the entrepreneur system. Prices, the document said, must in general be kept stable and profits must be kept broadly in line with an incomes policy, although the wonderful admission is made that "in a dynamic economy it is inevitable, and indeed desirable, that some prices should go up while others go down" and that "profits must vary from firm to firm and from industry to industry". The Government's argument was that more prices should have gone down "than has been the case in the past"—we all agree that an industry's prices should fall where productivity is increasing faster than the national average—and accordingly it asked the N.I.C. to adopt a more critical attitude towards profit margins. While it did not expect that changes in the rate of profit should necessarily be kept within the limits of the 3% to 3½% annual growth rate for earned incomes—as if they could!— it advised the N.I.C. to focus attention on prices, profit margins and rates of return on capital and suggested that it might relate total profits to the gross national product (after adjusting for changes in the number of firms or in the total of capital employed) to see if undue profits were in fact being made. The object of this simple statistical exercise was, I presume, to turn the N.I.C. into a price-reviewing as well as wage-reviewing body.

If this document had been the brain-child of a schoolboy debating society it would have been understandable, but coming from the Treasury in the eighteenth year after the death of Keynes it was intensely depressing. Small wonder that it provoked Enoch Powell into the other extreme of declaring that wages, prices and profits "always will be and always have been determined, until we go Communist, by supply and demand".

If Enoch Powell and the novice who wrote the Treasury document really wanted to know how prices were fixed they should have read the excellent piece of research done by Robert Neild, of the National Institute of Economic and Social Research, on *Pricing and Employment in the Trade Cycle*.[1] His findings confirm the theory set out by a senior Treasury official (W. A. H. Godley) in an unpublished paper, from which Robert Neild quoted as follows:

> "Businessmen have in their mind an idea about what the long-term trend of output is and fix their prices on the basis of the costs implied by the trend and keep them there when output fluctuates about the trend. So profit margins rise when output rises faster and fall when output rises less fast or declines."

It is as simple as that! Of course, there are occasions when prices are fixed too high. This usually happens when a great industrial combine has secured a virtual monopoly of the market and can charge what it likes without fear of competition. (Something of the sort has been seen in cables, in wallpaper and in some electrical appliances supplied to the motor industry.) The way to break these monopoly prices is by tough anti-monopoly and anti-trust legislation, as they do in America. In this country we can apply to the Restrictive Practices Court and the Monopolies Commission whose powers the Government is now extending.[2] But this is mild legislation by comparison with the American, and it is not without significance that the Government proposes to set up a Registrar of Monopolies to "ascertain the facts", so that companies do not feel that the Monopolies Commission is both "judge and prosecutor".

[1] Cambridge University Press, 1964.

[2] The Commission is to be given power to inquire into mergers and to make a monopoly firm divest itself of an interest, subject to the approval of Parliament, if required. The Restrictive Practices Court is to be empowered to register and make orders in respect of "information agreements", bilateral agreements and maximum price agreements which still operate to limit competition.

This Treasury document did have the fairness to warn the N.I.C. that a long-term view of profits was necessary. It added:

> "This is particularly relevant at the present time when company profits are recovering from the downturn experience in 1961 and 1962. It is still too soon to estimate how much further this recovery will go but there has been a fall in the relative share both of company profits and of aggregate profit incomes compared with aggregate earned incomes over the past ten years."

There has indeed been a fall and if you look back forty years you will find that it is almost a collapse. In the nineteen-twenties the share of "profit and interest" in the national income was a third; but in 1960-62 it was just under a fifth. Between 1950 and 1960 the annual percentage rise in gross profits was only 5·4% (and 3·6% for self-employed profits) against 7·1% in wages and salaries.

Stafford Cripps once told the trade unions that if company profits were mulcted of 25% it would mean an average addition to wages and salaries of no more than 4*d.* in the £. That is still more or less true today.

Keynes at one time used to talk happily of the coming euthanasia of the rentier, but if the trend line for declining profits is carried forward another ten or twenty years it will be necessary to speak of the euthanasia of the entrepreneur. An analysis of the rates of return on capital employed by companies suggests that this is no fanciful anticipation. Within the ten years to 1962 earnings on capital employed have fallen from 18·5% to approximately 12¼%. Admittedly 1962 was a bad year for comparison, thanks to the Lloydian squeeze, but even so it is a disturbing thought for the free-enterprise system that the profitability of capital should have dropped by a third since 1953.[1] Edward Heath not long ago confessed to a company of overseas bankers assembled at a Guildhall banquet that British companies would find it harder to earn profits as a result of his stiffening up of the law of monopolies and restrictive practices and the abolition of resale price maintenance. It is something

[1] Although American industry has also experienced a decline in profitability in this period, the rate of return on American industrial capital is much higher than on British—more than can be explained by the greater size of the American market.

INCOME AND ASSETS EMPLOYED OF QUOTED COMPANIES,[1] 1950-62

| | *Gross assets*[2] | *Gross income*[3] | | *Net assets* | *Net income*[4] | |
|---|---|---|---|---|---|---|
| | | | *as % gross assets* | | | *as % net assets* |
| | *£mn.* | *£mn.* | | *£mn.* | *£mn.* | |
| 1950 | 6,580 | 1,091 | 16·6 | 5,366 | 921 | 17·2 |
| 1951 | 7,333 | 1,301 | 17·8 | 6,011 | 1,111 | 18·5 |
| 1952 | 8,078 | 1,398 | 17·3 | 6,602 | 1,189 | 18·0 |
| 1953 | 8,767 | 1,554 | 17·7 | 7,125 | 1,320 | 18·5 |
| 1954 | 9,540 | 1,698 | 17·8 | 7,749 | 1,429 | 18·4 |
| 1955 | 10,458 | 1,798 | 17·0 | 8,499 | 1,502 | 17·7 |
| 1956 | 11,496 | 1,865 | 16·3 | 9,287 | 1,518 | 16·3 |
| 1957 | 12,620 | 1,986 | 15·7 | 10,121 | 1,593 | 15·7 |
| 1958 | 13,687 | 2,081 | 15·2 | 10,935 | 1,639 | 15·0 |
| 1959 | 14,840 | 2,313 | 15·6 | 11,808 | 1,827 | 15·5 |
| 1960 | 16,305 | 2,559 | 15·7 | 12,905 | 2,021 | 15·7 |
| 1961 | 17,634 | 2,393 | 13·6 | 13,701 | 1,823 | 13·3 |
| 1962 | 18,957 | 2,405 | 12·7 | 14,625 | 1,780 | 12·2 |

[1] Quoted companies engaged mainly in the United Kingdom in manufacturing, distribution, construction and transport, including subsidiaries acquired during the year.

[2] Net assets plus accumulated depreciation; average of figures at start and end of each year.

[3] Gross trading profits plus other income before tax; stock appreciation excluded.

[4] Gross income less depreciation; stock appreciation excluded.

Sources: *Statistics on Incomes, Prices, Employment and Labour April, 1962*; *Preliminary Estimates of National Income and Expenditure 1956-61*; *Board of Trade Journal.*

that he recognised that company profitability in this country is becoming more and more of a headache for the executives, but for an official Treasury document to boast of its critical attitude towards profit margins in order to propagate the myth that profits are part of an incomes policy was discreditable.

If Maudling ever seriously believed that he could get George Woodcock and his T.U.C. friends to agree to an N.E.D.C. statement advocating wage restraint in return for a phoney N.I.C. critique of company profits he must be a wiser man today.

## Dividends

Dividends, unlike profits, can be legislatively controlled and were, in fact, to be brought under statutory limitation by Hugh Gaitskell when he was Chancellor, but before the legislation could be passed the Tories were back in office. Harold Wilson has declared himself against the statutory limitation of dividends; he prefers to put a special tax on them if necessary. I hope he will not do so. A discriminatory tax on dividends would be harmful to the efficient working of the private sector of the economy. After Harold Macmillan had put up the tax on distributed profits to 27½% in 1956 there followed two years of stagnation. Business people did not become enterprising again until Amory had introduced a flat 10% profits tax in April 1958 (it is now 15%).

Of course Tory Chancellors called for restraint in dividends as they did for restraint in wages, but they made no attempt to enforce it and the appeal was obviously ignored. Directors continued to pay out in dividends the rate which they thought the market or the business required. I expect that some boards of directors have recently been paying out more than they need, so that if Labour comes into power and freezes dividends the distribution rate will be frozen at a high and not a low level. You cannot really blame them for that. But dividends are not a big item in the national accounts; they are only one-fourteenth of the total amount of wages and salaries; they are only one-fourth of gross company income; they are only 5½% of the national income.

## Salaries and Wages

As regards salaries, no serious attempt has ever been made to apply a guiding light to the white collar worker except Selwyn Lloyd's attempt to squeeze the salaries of teachers and nurses. Industrial and commercial salaries follow the annual or biennial rise which every management gives to its staff according to their advancing age or experience. Not even Selwyn Lloyd's pay pause put a stop to this hoary routine. As most managements do not err on the side of generosity to their staffs —bank clerks have evidence of that—no one has suggested that the conventional rise in salaries should have a stop or even a restraint.

So we come back to wages. Obviously it has not improved the temper of the trade unions to discover that the application of the "guiding light" to rents, profits, dividends and salaries has always been a pretence. To apply it to wages was from the outset an administrative impracticability and Maudling has only made it more impracticable by insisting that the rise in wages should not go ahead of the rise in productivity. This meant that the most efficient industries would have to deny their workers the rise to which their exceptional productivity entitled them, so that workers in other industries whose productivity was not rising could enjoy the 3½% rise allowed for the whole. I am well aware that Maudling will say that there is no need for any such Procustean rigidity—some industries, he says, can be allowed a bigger rise in wages than others—but this rigidity was emphatically stated by the National Incomes Commission in their July 1963 report to be an essential and vital part of a wages policy.[1] This is scarcely the way to further the growth of the national economy. In practice neither the managements, who want to hold on to efficient labour, nor the workers who want to secure the fruits of their extra skill and energy, would ever agree to such a proposal. The piece-workers would just down tools.

## Wage Rates and Drift

The pre-Maudling attempts at a wages policy were very crude. They amounted simply to putting a restraint or check upon nationally negotiated wage rates. And that on an annual basis. This was because the wage rate was the only component of the worker's earnings which seemed amenable to central control. The Government idea was that wage rates must not rise in any one year by such an amount as would cause wage earnings next year to exceed the permitted rate of growth. But this obviously had complications. A rate negotiated mid-year within the 3½% guiding light could easily lead to a rise next year in total wage incomes of well above 3½% while a 6% rise negotiated at the end of a year after a pause of eighteen months could be within the guiding light.

In their evidence which they submitted to the N.I.C. on the engineering wage settlement of 1963 two Oxford economists who have been conducting a research into wage problems for

[1] This report stated: "In the context of an incomes policy the notion that it is the right of every industry to appropriate for itself the whole of the fruits of its own greater productivity is mistaken and should be abandoned."

many years—K. G. J. C. Knowles and D. Robinson of the Oxford Institute of Economics and Statistics—laid great emphasis on the fact that restraint of wage rates in themselves would not necessarily avoid a rise in wage incomes ahead of the rise in productivity. While wage rates were one source of higher earnings they were far from being the only source or even at times the main source. This was recognised in the White Paper of February 1962 (*Incomes Policy: The Next Step*) but Knowles and Robinson went so far as to say that there was no adequate evidence to suggest that increases in wage earnings were uniquely associated with increases in wage rates. Total earnings can be more significantly affected by reductions in weekly hours, by productivity and incentive bonuses, by overtime (especially on Sundays at double rates), by "danger" money, by "dirty" money (working in unpleasant conditions), by "merit" rates, by special local allowances and compensation payments and so on. Overtime is often an organised phoney way of increasing weekly earnings. These experts give examples of the "gap"—the extent to which wage earnings have already drifted away from wage rates. In one case the "gap" was 47%. In engineering, they add, wage earnings have so far drifted away from rates that it is no longer sensible to concentrate on rates. The interim report of the N.I.C. (June 1964) on the engineering and shipbuilding settlement more or less adopted their point of view.

I think it is fair to conclude from the researches of Knowles and Robinson that any attempt by the N.I.C. to assess the "permissibility" of a particular increase in wage rates is futile because it can know nothing about the subsequent extent of the wage "drift". If the gap between wage rates and total wage earnings were to decline in percentage terms the rise in wage rates could legitimately exceed the guiding light, while if the gap were to increase, the rise in wage rates would have to be lower than the guiding light. In fact, no rise in wage rates would be permissible at all if "drift" had already gone beyond the guiding light. All this is proof of my contention that it was always impracticable to propose a guiding light for wages, let alone for incomes in general.

The whole wages structure of British industry is so complicated that it is bound to defeat any rational approach to a wages policy. It has grown up over many years by agreement between workers and managements and is now firmly established for the two main systems of payment—by time and by results. In each trade there is a wage rate related to a standard working week of so many hours, which tends to be a minimum rate, and there are supplementary rules which govern extra payments for working overtime, at inconvenient times, in difficult or dirty conditions, during lay-offs and for vacations. In some industries there are hybrid variations of this system of great variety. The whole structure is so complex that a single guiding light could never be applied. That is the conclusion I draw from the researches of the two Oxford economists whose evidence I have quoted.[1] Certainly they made it clear that Government intervention in the wages structure had really made things worse, because it had been so thoughtless. Kenneth Knowles concluded his study of wages in *The British Economy in the Nineteen-Fifties* with this opinion:

"Experience suggests that it is highly questionable whether the unions with their jealously guarded autonomy would agree to a formal national wages policy . . . if only on the grounds that a correspondingly radical policy on profits and prices would prove equally inacceptable to other parties."

## Are British Wages too High?

Was Reginald Maudling really disappointed when the T.U.C. representatives on N.E.D.C. in January 1964 refused to sign a joint declaration with the employers calling for restraint on prices and incomes? Did he really imagine that the workers would behave like Christian martyrs in a free-for-all competitive economy, the conduct of which they regard as immoral? The employers later admitted that a joint declaration was impracticable. Our society being split economically into two opposing interests, it must be expected that the workers will go on inflating their share of the available profits of private enterprise—until the point is reached when private enterprise is no longer interested in employing them. To those of us who are not organised workers the perpetual grab of the trade unions may appear reprehensible and at times anti-social but when we

[1] In a letter to *The Spectator* of 6th March 1964, Mr. Knowles and Mr. Robinson objected somewhat that I had drawn conclusions from their evidence rather more dismissive than they had intended to imply. To quote: "It may be that in the real world as he suggests an effective incomes policy will prove to be a myth. We are inclined to doubt this and although the prevailing ignorance of many details of wage payment must keep us agnostic we do not feel that it need of itself assure us of failure."

appreciate the struggle they have had against Government restraints to keep ahead of the rise in prices we should become more sympathetic. I have already referred in Part II to the fact under the Conservative régime up to the end of 1963 the workers won a rise in their real standard of living averaging 4% per annum against an average of 19% per annum in the real value of the equity shares owned by their employers. In an analysis which he made of wage claims between 1953 and 1961[1] Robinson found that in every year some groups of workers, on the basis of the rise they won in wage rates (not total earnings), actually had a fall in their real incomes. Of the total of 147 groups analysed 98 had a fall in at least one year, 30 had falls in two years, 7 in three years and 3 in four years. In 1961, the year of the pay pause, 54 groups—37% of the total—suffered a decline in real incomes. So it cannot be said that the organised workers by refusing the policy of wage restraint have got away with enormous gains. They have had a hard struggle to achieve a modest rise in their standard of living.

AVERAGE HOURLY WAGE COSTS IN MANUFACTURING INDUSTRY. APRIL 1959

| | *Hourly wage cost $* | *Basic wage %* | *Social charges %* | *Supplementary labour costs[3] as % of 1st col.* |
|---|---|---|---|---|
| U.S.A. | 2.68 | 83 | 17 | 22·5 |
| Sweden | 1.08 | 87 | 13 | 15·3 |
| Germany | 0.78 | 69 | 31 | 44·3 |
| Switzerland | 0.77 | 87 | 13 | 15·4 |
| U.K. | 0.77 | 88 | 12 | 14.0 |
| Belgium | 0.74 | 76 | 24 | 31·0 |
| France | 0.71 | 66 | 34 | 50·0[2] |
| Italy | 0.61 | 57 | 43 | 74·0 |
| Holland | 0.57 | 77 | 23 | 30·1 |

[1] Vol. 25 of the *Bulletin of the Oxford Institute of Statistics*, February 1963.

[2] Includes 5·2% payroll tax.

[3] Includes in addition to social security, family allowances (except in case of U.S.A., U.K. and Sweden), holiday pay, bonuses and welfare payments (house, etc.). Family allowances in the case of France and Italy are as high as 16·2% and 20½% respectively.

Source: French National Institute of Statistics and Economic Studies.

It will be seen from the above table that British wages are still far behind American and not far out of line with European. Indeed, the British employer does not have to bear the heavy charges for social security and welfare with which the French, German and Italian employers are loaded. To the up-to-date American industrialist, British labour still seems cheaply hired. The universal trend is towards higher wages and fewer working hours in every advanced industrial country of the capitalist world. How else do you suppose that the capitalist world could convince the workers that the communist system is not better? If Khruschev thinks that the workers' choice between the two systems will be decided by a purely material calculation we must try to work out the sum so that it ends in our favour.

## Growth

The realisation at long last that an incomes policy would never be agreed to, that the workers would never behave like gentlemen in a capitalist society which they regarded as an ungentlemanly "free-for-all", made the more enlightened members of the Conservative Party extremely anxious to promote growth and even willing after ten years of office in a make-believe free economy to accept a degree of State planning in the interests of growth. How else, they asked, could industry afford the rise in wages which the logic of social history, not to mention the bargaining power of the big trade unions, made inevitable?

The trouble had been in the past that successive Tory Chancellors had harboured such widely different notions about growth. Butler had appeared to leave it vaguely to the natural growth of population and productivity, but he stirred the public imagination when he said that we could double our standard of living within a generation.[1] Unfortunately Thorneycroft, who followed him, put growth second to hard money. A strong £, he said, must come before full employment. Amory agreed. He remarked on one occasion that faster economic growth should not be attempted in advance of the other objectives of economic policy, namely, a sound balance of payments and stable prices. Selwyn Lloyd in his neurotic attempt to stop the rise in wages succeeded in stopping growth altogether. But he had left behind him the National Economic Development Council which, with Maudling as chairman, began to take growth very seriously. Its objects were defined as follows:

[1] Increased productivity is the key. If output fails to keep pace with the increase in population the result is a lowering of living standards.

(*a*) to examine the economic performance of the nation with particular concern for plans for the future in both the private and the public sectors of industry.
(*b*) to consider together what are the obstacles to quicker growth, what can be done to improve efficiency and whether the best use is being made of our resources.
(*c*) to seek agreement upon ways of improving economic performance, competitive power and efficiency: in other words, to increase the rate of sound growth.

Its first report, published in February 1963 under the title of "Growth of the U.K. Economy to 1966" settled on 4% as the growth rate objective. That was no doubt a helpful start in the job of educating the public to become more growth-conscious. Its second report, published in April 1963, was entitled "Conditions Favourable to Faster Growth". It discussed education, mobility and redundancy of labour, regional questions, balance of payments policies and taxation, but it arrived at extremely conventional conclusions about the need for a high level of demand and an incomes policy. "To aim at a level of employment in 1966 substantially above the level of 1962" was hardly a stimulating call for three years' growth.

The Council may well have asked themselves whether the easy-going British way of life would tolerate a much faster rate of growth. Certainly we could improve on our past record. Growth in the standard of living is usually measured in terms of the gross national product per head of the population. The U.S.A. have the highest standard of living in the world, for their G.N.P. is equivalent to nearly £800 per head. Sweden comes next with £583. We have sunk to third place with £455. And we will not keep this place if we do not better the performance we have put up since 1938.

There is no simple explanation of our shocking performance in the growth league other than the fact that our stupid economic policies of dear money and "stop-go-stop", which Conservative Chancellors applied in the interests of the balance of payments, have continually restricted normal growth while our lack of central planning and of scientific expertise allowed private enterprise to go on year after year adding to industrial investment of the wrong sort.

Of course, some allowance has to be made for our island peculiarities. West Germany, Italy and France have had a

NATIONAL GROWTH RATES: ANNUAL AVERAGE COMPOUND PER CENT. RATES OF CHANGE

| | *Real Gross National Product* | | | *Real National Product per man-year* | | |
|---|---|---|---|---|---|---|
| *Table* | *1938-61* | *1950-55* | *1955-61* | *1938-61* | *1950-55* | *1955-61* |
| W. Germany | 3·7% | 9·1% | 6·0% | 2·3% | 6·0% | 3·5% |
| France | 2·6 | 4·5 | 4·3 | 2·6 | 4·3 | 3·5 |
| Italy | 3·0 | 6·0 | 5·8 | 2·3 | 5·4 | 4·1 |
| Holland | 3·3 | 5·7 | 4·0 | 1·7 | 4·4 | 2·6 |
| U.S.A | 4·2 | 4·3 | 2·2 | 2·2 | 2·8 | 1·4 |
| U.K. | 1·8 | 2·8 | 2·2 | 1·0 | 1·8 | 1·6 |

more elastic supply of labour, let alone a greater rise in population. Germany has had the benefit of an influx of refugees from East Germany, while Italy has been able to tap the reservoir of unemployed labour in the south. Also, there has been a much larger shift in labour from agriculture to industry in those countries where a larger proportion of the population was employed on the farms than in Britain. Again, the different proportions of labour employed in agriculture, manufacturing and consumer services must lead to different productivity increases. In a country like Britain, where services form an increasingly important part of the national product, productivity expressed over the whole labour force would naturally rise more slowly than in countries where services played a less important part in output. The statistics are not corrected for these differences. Even so, when allowance has been made for them, the U.K. would still come out at the bottom of the table.

The O.E.C.D. and the E.E.C. have been doing a lot of statistical work on this subject and have re-calculated the productivity figures on the assumption that each country had the same employment movements from one sector to another and the same standard output structure—the same division of resources as between agriculture, manufacturing and services. This re-calculation raised Britain's productivity record in the decade 1949-59 up from 20% to 24% and the American from 23% to 32%, but these are still well below those of Germany and Italy—57% and 52% respectively—after applying the same standard. The fact that population grew more rapidly in Germany and Italy than in the U.K. does not seem to make much difference. If output is expressed per man-year we are still at the bottom. So I am afraid that while the table can be re-written to make the comparison a little less awful for the U.K., it is still awful enough.

It is sometimes argued in our favour that the Continental countries started from a much lower level of output than the U.K.—having been hit more severely by bombing and bombardment—and had the advantage of using much more new equipment. But this argument does not necessarily work to our credit. One might have expected that after the Continental countries had passed their pre-war levels of output their rate of increase in productivity would slow down, but in fact it has not done so. The efficiency of their new capital equipment has improved their rate of progress.

## Investment and the Rate of Growth

Why did we not re-equip our own industries as far and as efficiently as our competitors? It was not merely a question of stepping up the proportion of the national income applied to investment. In the great investment boom the U.K. did in fact increase its investment ratio. It went up from 14% to 17½% between 1954 and 1961 and to 18½% in 1962. Even so it was still below the proportion of the national income applied to investment in some other countries—for example 20½% in Sweden and 24% in Germany. But this investment effort in the U.K. led to no perceptible increase in the growth rate of productivity. Indeed, Blackaby, whose paper on "The Recent Performance of the British Economy" I have quoted, brings out the disconcerting fact that the advanced countries which have shown the slowest growth in the post-war period, namely Britain, the U.S.A., Canada and Belgium, have invested more in relation to their rise in output than the countries which have grown faster—France, Germany, Italy and the Netherlands. Our own rate of increase of capital per worker has been very nearly the same as in France: yet the French productivity record is almost twice as high.

The table on p. 141 which reveals these discrepancies is taken from J. R. Sargent's excellent Fabian Tract No. 343 on *A Policy for Growth*.

There are two explanations of the lack of correlation between capital accumulation and the rate of growth. First, the pattern of investment in slow growing countries has not been well designed for producing the maximum increase in output, in

ANNUAL AVERAGE RATE OF GROWTH 1950-60

| | *G.N.P. per employee* | *Capital stock per employee* | (1) *as ratio of* (2) |
|---|---|---|---|
| W. Germany | 5·0 | 4·6 | 1·09 |
| France | 3·9 | 3·0 | 1·30 |
| Holland | 3·6 | 3·5 | 1·03 |
| Sweden | 3·3 | 1·7 | 1·93 |
| Norway | 3·1 | 4·9 | 0·63 |
| Belgium | 2·4 | 2·6 | 0·92 |
| U.K. | 2·1 | 2·9 | 0·72 |
| U.S.A. | 1·9 | 2·8 | 0·60 |

other words, it has been the wrong sort of investment and not labour-saving enough. Secondly, as the case of Britain demonstrates, a growing under-utilisation of potential capacity is bound to follow upon dear money, "stop-go-stop" policies and too slow a growth of demand, not to mention the immobility of labour, the restrictionism of trade union practices and other troubles with labour over redundancy.

Maudling must have appreciated this investment problem when he sharply increased the investment allowances in his 1963 budget but he made the mistake of continuing to make these allowances indiscriminate, so that they can be secured equally by companies whose investment is not of a labour-saving sort. Here surely is the main cause of the slow growth of output in the U.K. And once again it stems from the inept financial policies of the Conservative Chancellors.

## Investment Planning

Industrial investment in this country has been concerned too much with securing the financial profit of the investment allowances, that is with tax saving, and too little with the introduction of new industrial techniques and the saving of labour through automation. It is what you would expect when the top people running British industry have been for the most part finance-capitalists lacking in technical expertise, the practical men of the old fashioned type with family or "old school tie" connections.[1] These financial gentlemen lose no chance of securing the investment allowance for mere expansion of capacity or the duplication of existing plant just to

[1] Where these types are not available it is common practice to invite to the chairman's seat an accountant or an ex-civil servant with a title, which is even worse.

increase their equity share earnings. The quality of industrial investment must always suffer if a taxation bribe is offered without scrutiny of the purpose of the investment.

The encouragement of indiscriminate investment was carried a stage further last year when the Government offered new inducements to business people to set up in the development districts where there is high unemployment. Under the Local Employment Act of 1963 the Board of Trade has power to offer standard grants of 25% of building costs and 10% of plant and machinery in addition to the other forms of assistance under the 1960 Act. And under the Finance Act of 1963 the Treasury allowed the businessman to write off his capital expenditure in qualifying plant and machinery at whatever rate he chooses. The Boards of Trade and Inland Revenue actually issued a pamphlet reminding business people going into the development districts that under these joint schemes they can recover up to 73% of the cost of qualifying plant and machinery within two years (60% in the first year) and up to 71% of the cost of the building over the life of the asset (34% in the first year).[1] The local "development" districts may benefit from this State bribery but the nation as a whole will be saddled with more and more industrial investment which does not advance our competitive position in the world markets.

Yet our industrial future really depends on improving that competitiveness. Why were the Conservative Chancellors so complacent about it? Simply because it was against their tenets to impose any form of central Whitehall control over business activity. When I put the question of control of investment allowances to the Chancellor of the Exchequer in his private room at the House of Commons in 1962 he seemed horrified at

[1] Here is an illustration:

| | | | | |
|---|---|---|---|---|
| Year I | (*a*) Standard grant of 10% of cost of acquisition and installation | 10·0% | | |
| | (*b*) Tax Savings: investment allowance 30% of 90% at 10/9 in £, income tax 7/9 and property tax 15% | 14·5 | | |
| | Free depreciation 100% of 90% at 7/9 income tax | 34·9 | = | 59·4 |
| Year II | Tax savings: free depreciation 100% of 90% against profits tax of 15% | | | 13·5 |
| | | | | 72·9 |
| | Borne by owners | | | 27·1 |
| | | | | 100·0 |

the thought. Perhaps he felt that the civil servants who would have to administer such a control would be technically ill-qualified to do so. Or perhaps he secretly subscribed to the *laissez faire* principles of his ex-colleague Enoch Powell who really believes that everything can be left to the decision of the market-place.

Duncan Burn, who was formerly industrial correspondent of *The Times* and now heads a research institute for the heavy electrical industry, has been pointing out in articles and papers over many years that a large proportion of British industrial investment in the inter-war and post-war periods has been of a kind not likely to minimise costs or make the most of the opportunities offered by modern technology. He has given examples in steel, coal, gas, electrical generation, heavy and light electrical engineering, petro-chemicals, railways, ports, motor-cars and cotton. When an industrial expert of his long experience makes this criticism it should be taken seriously. Against the British achievements of the jet engine, the hovercraft, penicillin, the Pilkington plate glass process and the reduction of bauxite, he has drawn up a formidable list of industrial developments which we have either missed entirely or copied late from other countries, for example, the transistor, diesel electric motors, synthetic rubbers, low pressure polythene, polypropylene, acrylic fibres, the development of new metals and a host of improvements to motor-cars, packaging techniques, building methods, metal refining and mining technology. He attributes this failure to lack of "the intellectual elements of production", that is, to the lack of scientific knowledge among directors and managers and their apparent lack of interest in innovation. We always come back to the deadly, non-creative mind of finance-capitalism which has been the curse of Great Britain.

Having regard to the miserably poor quality of a lot of industrial investment in our country I was not surprised to read in the *Sunday Times* of March 1964 an article by an American management consultant, W. W. Allen, who has lived and worked here for the past six years, claiming that virtually every worker in British industry is under-employed, that basic wages and salaries are too low, that the normal work-week is too long, that overtime is unnecessary, that there is a potential "vast surplus" of labour but an insufficient supply of the right capital equipment and that the existing equipment is under-employed because the labour is under-employed. He believes that the capital equipment required can be manufactured and then operated by managers and workers set free by the increased productivity of the other members of the labour force and that it is possible to obtain this proper balance between labour and equipment in ten to fifteen years provided the accepted growth rate is at least double the 4% adopted by the N.E.D.C. In support of his thesis he quotes many facts from which I pick out three relating to our major industries. (1) Steel: for each man needed to produce a ton of steel in America three are needed in Britain; (2) Shipbuilding: ships could be built here with about 40% fewer men if labour were employed efficiently; (3) Building: it takes three to six times as long to build a house in Britain as it does in America. W. W. Allen was the consultant to the Esso refinery at Fawley which was able to reduce the size of the work force to below that in 1938 in spite of a £25 million capital expansion programme.[1]

### The Planning Machinery

Obviously, the sort of industrial revolution we require is impossible without much more intelligent planning of industrial investment, much more application of science to industry, much wider use of university-trained technicians and scientists in company managements—and perhaps more employment of American industrial consultants. Is the N.E.D.C. the right body to give this lead?

The French have been able to carry out an industrial revolution on the initiative of their own State Commissariat du Plan—without the help of American experts. This Commissariat was born in the revolutionary days after the liberation of a nation rescued from death to the peaceful task of industrial reconstruction and modernisation. It combined French patriotic fervour with French brains. It set up a Modernisation Commission consisting of thirty to fifty industrialists, trade unionists and officials from the departments to plan the capital development for each sector of the economy. A final version of the plan, synthesising the sector studies, was drawn up for the approval of the Government. The staff of the Commissariat are civil servants but they are not part of the Ministry of Finance or tainted with the mildew of the financial mind. They are not the academic type of civil servants we use in Britain. They have all had some industrial or technical training and experience and they talk to the industrialists in their own

[1] See A. Flanders on "The Fawley Productivity Agreements".

language. They play an independent role and are the link between industry and Government. They have therefore been more persuasive than coercive. In fact, they have been able to persuade the industrialists to agree to five-year investment plans embodying the most up-to-date industrial techniques in the world. They have put France in the forefront of European industry.

By comparison our own N.E.D.C. is an amateurish body with a staff recruited from industry, the Civil Service and the universities (academic economists) but not from industrial technicians of the W. W. Allen type. Perhaps this is due to its different origin. It was born in the 1961 pay pause and was conceived mainly as a means of rescuing the Conservative Party from its labour crisis. I doubt whether it can survive in its present form. It is not yet clear, writes Duncan Burn in Unilever's magazine *Progress*, "whether in the end the N.E.D.C. will be one of those bodies created to do things specified in *general terms* 'in the national interest'—without any guiding (technical) criteria." Its first investment "target" was simply dreamed up by its academic staff but it is now setting up industrial commissions to plan the investment of nine industries—chemicals, distributive trades, confectionery, electrical engineering, electronics, machine tools, mechanical engineering, paper and board, woollen textiles. Of these nine little N.E.D.C.s which were expected last autumn five only have been established as I write in June 1964: and none has yet got down to work. On the success or failure of these industrial commissions the N.E.D.C. will stand or fall.

The Opposition has, of course, tumbled to these shortcomings and has sworn to put a reformed N.E.D.C. on its feet and on its job. Harold Wilson has condemned the indiscriminate investment allowances and local bribes. He has promised to be "ruthless" in his tax discrimination, giving the investment allowances only to those firms which install automation and other labour-saving devices, which boost exports or save imports by the introduction of new industrial techniques.[1] Presumably investment allowances would not be available for companies making luxury goods for the home market. As the application of science to industry was made the theme of last year's Labour Party Conference it can be assumed that industrial investment, if it is to claim a subsidy from the State, will have to be more scientifically planned under a Labour Government and

[1] See his Swansea speech, January 1964.

directed specifically towards export boosting or import saving. Wilson seems to be contemplating a kind of French Commissariat du Plan with more technicians, fewer civil servants, with rather less persuasion in it and rather more State direction.

The Conservative Government's answer to the urgent call for more scientific and better-planned investment is simply to rely on the good effects of more competition in a free market. In the White Paper it has recently issued on monopolies, mergers and restrictive practices, it claims that "competition has an essential role to play both in stimulating innovation and efficiency". This is not to be denied and the proposals it is making for strengthening and extending the field of its legislation on monopolies and restrictive practices and bringing to an end resale price maintenance (except where exemption is granted by the Restrictive Practices Court) will certainly help. But they are not enough. What do they amount to but a mild supervision of the inevitable trend towards mergers and monopolies? To quote Duncan Burn again: "It is a complete fallacy to suppose that competition always puts things right in conditions of oligopoly. I believe it is impossible for the forces of competition left to themselves rapidly to remove the handicaps imposed by an obsolete (industrial) infrastructure."

We have all become far too complacent about our industrial future. The present wide scatter of our industries and ports, which grew up down the years of our first industrial revolution, is now a positive handicap to our manufacturing efficiency and to our competitive position in the world markets.

It is certainly not wise to imagine that the second industrial revolution we require will be brought about either by the free play of competition among the oligopolies and their little rivals, enforced by a little more bite from the Monopolies Commission and the Restrictive Practices Court, or by free enterprise investment prompted only by a somewhat academic N.E.D.C. and substantial bribes from the State. No one—not even the N.E.D.C.—has yet begun to re-plan the industrial infrastructure on a national scale. We remain what that rude American consultant called us: "A half-time country getting half-pay for half-work under half-hearted management."

### Cheap Money

It will be impossible to carry out the industrial reconstruction of this country at the high rate of interest which the

Conservative Chancellors have imposed on the market. The cost would be prohibitive at over 6%.

Money is like manure: it does most good when it is spread widely and cheaply over the many fertile fields of the national economy. When it is costly, when it is in short supply, the only people who benefit are the owners and managers of it, the bankers and financiers, for then they can put up its price—the rate of interest—and make a "killing". If only these parasitic gentlemen who trade in our savings and deposits would regard themselves as humble manure-spreaders on the national farm and not lift up their voices at their annual bank meetings and tell us how the farm should be run!

Dalton was right to insist on cheap money in 1945. He had to service a much heavier load of Government debt after the war (up from £7,000 million to £24,000 million) and carry out a huge social investment in houses and flats, schools and hospitals. For all these public purposes it was essential that money should be cheap. With the sterling deposits of our overseas creditors at £3,500 million and our floating debt of Treasury bills at £6,000 million every unnecessary extra 1% on the interest bill would have meant that the already overburdened tax-payer would have to pay £60 million more in debt service at home and £35 million in debt service abroad—not to mention 10/- a week more in rent if he happened to live in a new Council house. It was a splendid achievement of Dalton to get the banks to lend day-to-day money to the Government on £6,000 million of Treasury bills and "deposit receipts" at ½% per annum. The service of the floating debt has never been so cheaply provided for—before or since. Under Dalton it was a mere £30 million a year: under Conservative Chancellors who believed in dear money, £200 million a year!

It was a great pity that Dalton gave cheap money a bad name by carrying it too far and applying it to every speculative Tom, Dick and Harry. The conversion of 3½ Local Loans in January 1947 into the undated Treasury 2½% ("Daltons") was a tactical mistake. Before the end of that year it had become clear that the market was not willing to accept 2½% as a long-term rate. It took fright when it saw that the Treasury was only holding the rate by flooding the joint stock banks with money through an increase in the Treasury bill issue. (Bank deposits had actually risen by £830 million in 1946, of which £600 million had gone into the gilt-edged market.) A flood of selling developed and although the Government departments bought (net) £570 million of Government stocks in the fifteen months ending March 1948—acquiring over half the entire issue of "Daltons"—the public had sold £630 million. The "bears" had won and Dalton was beaten.

Do not blame Dalton too much. He was no expert technician. He depended upon his Treasury advisers and in Volume 3 of his memoirs he has told us that he was getting much encouragement in his cheap money policy "from the top brass both at the Bank and the Treasury". He actually gave the names of the technicians responsible for the 2½% operation—Catto and Cobbold at the Bank, Bridges, Hopkins and Compton at the Treasury and Bampton at the Inland Revenue. No doubt his vanity had been tickled by the thought of out-doing Goschen. In his famous speech in the Commons, when calling 3% Local Loans for redemption, he referred to Goschen's attack on his 3% in 1888 (when 2½% Consols were created) and boasted that, unlike himself, Goschen never secured a better market rate than 2¾%. Pride as usual went before the fall. But I do not believe that Dalton ever understood the true market position. Dominating as he was, he would never deliberately have overridden his experts on a technical matter. He subsequently told me that he had had misgivings about an undated stock and would have preferred a dated stock redeemable in A.D. 2000 so that he could make a few parliamentary jokes about the date. But the money technicians had misjudged the market[1] and had given him the wrong advice. They might have held the long-term rate at 3½%, but 2½% was plainly untenable at the time.

I had discussed all this in an article in *The Spectator* of 23rd February 1962, which I sent to Hugh Gaitskell for his comment. I had this interesting letter in reply (dated 6th March 1962) which I have Lady Gaitskell's permission to reproduce:

> "I entirely agree with all that you say. In particular, that Hugh was absolutely right to go out for cheap money, that he went too far, but that this was very definitely on the advice of the Treasury experts.

[1] They had made a mistake in issuing short-dated 2½% Savings Bonds 1964-67 at too cheap a price in May 1946 after a steep rise in market prices. This upset the morale of the market and caused prices to fall heavily. Dalton referred to it in his autobiography as "Cobbold's slip-up".

"It is perhaps worth pointing out that even by 1951, interest rates were still comparatively low although I was prepared to let the long-term rate go up to 4%. The really crucial change, however, came with the removal of the 'peg' which the Bank wanted to do, which I had refused to do, and which the Tories did almost immediately after they came into power."

Before Gaitskell left office in 1951 the long-term rate had risen to 3¾%. Within ten years it had jumped to over 6%. Running the country at 6%, which is virtually what the Conservatives have done, has put up our industrial costs, weakened our competitive position, slowed down our rate of growth and added to the burden of taxation. That extra 2% added appreciably to our cost of living.

Here is the Conservative money record since Bank rate was loosed from its 2% anchor.

| | | | |
|---|---|---|---|
| Nov. 8, 1951 | 2½% | Nov. 20, 1958 | 4% |
| Mar. 11, 1952 | 4% | Jan. 21, 1960 | 5% |
| Sept. 17, 1953 | 3½% | June 23, 1960 | 6% |
| May 13, 1954 | 3% | Oct. 27, 1960 | 5½% |
| Jan. 27, 1955 | 3½% | Dec. 8, 1960 | 5% |
| Feb. 24, 1955 | 4½% | July 26, 1961 | 7% |
| Feb. 16, 1956 | 5½% | Oct. 5, 1961 | 6½% |
| Feb. 7, 1957 | 5% | Nov. 2, 1961 | 6% |
| Sept. 19, 1957 | 7% | Mar. 8, 1962 | 5½% |
| Mar. 20, 1958 | 6% | Mar. 22, 1962 | 5% |
| May 22, 1958 | 5½% | April 26, 1962 | 4½% |
| June 19, 1958 | 5% | Jan. 3, 1963 | 4% |
| Aug. 14, 1958 | 4½% | Feb. 27, 1964 | 5% |

Does this table not reveal the lunacy of the Bank rate merry-go-round? How can business people plan their investment programmes or their stock-building or their sales campaigns when the cost of borrowing is making so many erratic moves up and down—when the financial climate is turning from fair to foul or from foul to fair as capriciously as the British weather? Does the Government seriously expect the economy to show steady growth when it makes twenty-six changes in Bank rate in twelve years?

Why did they do it? Simply because they felt that if they gave up specific physical controls they must have what they called the "discipline" of dear money and tight credit to keep the economy under general restraint. The idea that discipline had to be applied to bodies like the local authorities over which they had direct spending control was of course ludicrous, but monetary discipline acquired a religious aura[1]—like flagellation —and had to be applied to everyone by the sado-masochists at the Treasury.

I would liken the Treasury disciplinarians to a lot of old-fashioned doctors trying to cure lunacy by whipping their patients in the mad-house—and not only the patients but the nurses as well! (Witness the huge rise in the Consolidated Fund bill as evidence of self-flagellation.) The Conservatives really believed that the discipline of dear money and tight credit would keep a wage-cost inflation in check. It took them twelve years to realise that while monetary deflation might damp down demand and depress the economy, it would never stop wages from rising.

### Bringing the Rate of Interest Down

The next Labour Government will have to bring the price of money down but it is not likely to repeat Dalton's mistakes. It will have to apply one rate of interest to social investment (housing, hospitals, schools, etc.) and another rate to the business community. I am not advocating a two-tier system of interest rates as a new technique for the money market. I am merely suggesting that the next Labour Government should finance the new towns and the local authorities by letting them have money at the rate the Treasury borrows on Treasury bills (which, as I write, is much too high at 4·4%, but with a reasonable Bank rate of 3½% could be brought down to 3%). The only borrower who can safely borrow short and lend long is the State, for it has ultimate control over all our incomes, our spending and our saving and can always get the debt repaid by a stroke of the budget pen.

If we could hold a 3% rate of interest for social investment what rate could we secure for business? I admit that while capital is allowed to move freely around the capitalist world it would be difficult to maintain a rate of interest much lower than that prevailing abroad, especially that in the United States. But the next Labour Government should impose some limitation on the in-flow of "hot money". It would have to do what the Swiss have done, which is to refuse to pay any

[1] See page 72 for Sir Robert Hall's comment on monetary magic.

interest on unwanted foreign deposits. It would also have to do what the late President Kennedy proposed, which is to restrain the issue of foreign securities in the domestic capital market. This would annoy the merchant banks in the City—especially Sir George Bolton of the Bank of London and South America who wants to make London the financial capital of the western world—but it is time that our industrial needs were given priority over banking luxuries.

If adequate measures were taken to insulate and protect the British capital market we could proceed to bring down the domestic rate of interest to a level which would encourage both private and public investment. This is important for purposes of growth, for if interest rates are kept too high for long industrial investment tends to decline and personal savings tend to rise faster than they can be put to work in actual capital spending. Selwyn Lloyd made the egregious mistake of raising the rate of interest at a time when personal savings were actually increasing faster than private enterprise investment. He did not seem to realise that he was thereby accentuating the slump in the capital goods industries.

The Conservative Chancellors seemed to proceed on the assumption that there was a permanent excess of demand for capital over the supply and that the rate of interest must therefore be kept permanently high in order to restrain it. Indeed they subscribed to the outmoded theory—even Maudling confessed it when I asked him the question—that investment and savings could only be brought into balance at the "equilibrium" rate of interest. If there were ever a free market the "equilibrium" rate would on occasion have to be so high —say 20%—as to be insupportable and impossible, but of course a free market economy no longer exists except in the minds of the hard money fanatics and Enoch Powell.

The Conservative Chancellors never understood the savings-investment equation. In the national accounts there is a statistical identity between total gross savings (surpluses of income over expenditure for persons, companies and State) and total gross investment (total expenditure on fixed and floating assets after allowing for investment or disinvestment overseas, that is, the surplus or deficit on the balance of payments). In practice business investment must rise or fall with profits and is, in fact, regulated by profits, while social investment is regulated by Central Government planning.

The approach of the next Labour Government to the question of money and its price will therefore be quite different from the market approach of the Conservatives. It will endeavour to plan a balance in the real capital account of the nation by drawing up a balance sheet showing the amount of the national resources available in plant and labour, plus imports, and the amount of money demand which can be allowed against them. It will try to match the capital account with the savings account and will cut down its public capital programme as well as the private in order to avoid any inflationary gap. The rate of interest will not enter into these calculations except for accounting purposes when estimates of profit or loss have to be worked out to see if an investment project is supportable. As the next Labour Government is not going to run a completely socialist state but a mixed economy, it will have to choose a rate of interest which is reasonable for the private sector and stimulating enough for its investment programme. This rate, I suggest, could be 4%.

It would be quite easy to secure a long-term rate of interest of 4% in the open market. As every economist knows, the level of the rate of interest depends on the relation of the volume of money supply to the national income, that is, to the national requirements for the use of money. By keeping the money supply restricted relative to the work it had to do the Conservative régime brought about this fantastic rise in the long-term rate of interest—from 3% to 6½%. Its technique was to go on feeding the market with long-dated stock while running down its supply of shorter-dated stock and Treasury bills. It was obsessed by these "funding" operations and the gilt-edged market was never allowed to rise to its normal level. To reverse this process the next Labour Government would have to abandon funding for a time and increase the supply of Treasury bills. It need not go as far as Dalton did, which is shown in the next table, but an increase of up to £500 million in the supply of Treasury bills, now floating at around £4,500 million, would probably do the trick. And it would be normal, not reckless, finance.

In the course of time we may rid ourselves of the curse of the rate of interest and for domestic purposes simply pay fees to bankers for the use of their funds. Keynes looked forward to the euthanasia of the rentier. According to Roy Harrod, his biographer, he departed in later years from this extreme opinion but never retreated from the view that interest rates should be kept low. This, I hope, will be the policy of the next Labour Government.

U.K. NATIONAL INCOME, BANK DEPOSITS AND YIELD ON $2\frac{1}{2}\%$ CONSOLS

| | *National income* £*mn.* | *Net bank deposits* £*mn.* | % *of* (1) | *Yield on* $2\frac{1}{2}\%$ *Consols* |
|---|---|---|---|---|
| 1938 | 5,175 | 2,277 | 44 | 3·3% |
| 1947 | 9,414 | 5,454 | 58 | 2·7% |
| 1963 | 26,331 | 8,565 | $32\frac{1}{2}$ | 5·5% |
| 1964 (mid.) | 26,900 (est) | 8,711 | $32\frac{1}{3}$ | 6·0% |

What a relief it will be to get our economic objectives in the right order! Growth, full employment, stable prices, balance of payments and exchange equilibrium—the Conservatives always gave top priority to the last two instead of to the first two. They insisted on high interest rates in order to draw foreign money to London to sustain the fixed gold-dollar rate for the £. Being finance-capitalists they were unable to put first things first. First things are human beings, their livelihood, their welfare and their happiness. But they put hard money first: the interest of the human people who use the stuff came second.

The financial and monetary policy which the Conservatives pursued was really founded on an illusion. The more they deflated, the greater the inflation. The more they stabilised, the greater the imbalance. The more they exacted forced savings from the public,[1] the more the people spent. In this curious universe there seems to be a law of action and reaction which applies as much to the monetary world as to Hoyle's world of particles. The higher the price of money the higher the price of goods. The greater the burden of debt the higher will prices rise to offset it. [In real terms the value of the inflated national debt today is much the same as it was in 1938.] The truth seems to be that money in wrong hands is an instrument of evil which not only destroys itself but destroys the people who worship it.

[1] For the nine years to 1962-63 the Conservative Chancellors exacted forced savings from the public at the rate of £357 million a year. That was the average annual size of the budget surplus.

# PART IV

# RESOLVING THE SOCIAL CONFLICT

SIXTEEN

# CAN LABOUR SATISFY THE EMPLOYERS?

ANOTHER GENERAL election approaches as I write and the expectation of a Labour victory has caused the trade union and parliamentary Labour leaders to come closer together on an incomes policy. Ted Hill has conceded that you cannot get more than a pint out of a pint pot.[1] Frank Cousins has admitted that if the economy is to be planned and the rate of growth stepped up, the trade unions cannot expect to be left out of the planning, in other words, that they must not count on unplanned wage increases in excess of economic growth. He would never agree to such an incomes policy under a Conservative Government, but if Labour is returned he would accept some restraint of wages provided other incomes—profits, dividends and rents—were also subjected to restraint. Is this possible? Does this mean that the division in society between ruling clique and working class will be closed if and when the next Labour Government takes office? Or widened further if the Conservatives are returned?

Certainly Harold Wilson would seem to have a greater chance to bring about the miraculous union than the ex-fourteenth Earl of Home. He has the right background—a nonconformist industrial origin, grammar-school education, a scholarship to Oxford followed by an economics fellowship. He has imbibed the modern scientific approach to the technological revolution which is required of British industry. Brains and hard work, not social pull, have brought him to the top. In the past all that was necessary for even a nonentity to reach the top in politics was to have come from the right family, to have been to the right school and to have had a pleasant disposition. That has been the trouble with the British political system—nice ineffectual people were always getting to the top. Such an absurdity happens less frequently in Russia.

[1] At the Boilermakers' Society conference in May 1964 Ted Hill remarked: "Nothing annoys me more than winning a wage increase only see it whittled away by increased prices. We should concentrate on a policy of price reduction." He proposed a wage freeze in return for a higher employers' contribution to national insurance to help the pensioners and the sick.

For the first time the employers would find themselves able to come to terms with a Labour Prime Minister whose approach to business is scientific rather than dogmatic and doctrinal. They could not have co-operated with his predecessors because of the Marxist Clause 4. Wilson is, in fact, the first Labour leader who can offer a mixed economy with which the capitalist can co-operate. This is due to the hard, plodding work of Hugh Gaitskell who believed passionately in the moderate socialism which Continental Europe had adopted after the war. The Socialist International in Frankfurt in 1951 passed this resolution: "Socialist planning does not presuppose the ownership of all the means of production. It is compatible with private ownership in important fields." That was Gaitskell's view and he tried to impose it on his party. He was determined to stamp out the nationalisation threats of the 1918 and 1945 policy memoranda which had been alarming and upsetting the private sector of the economy. In fact, he wanted Clause 4 abolished altogether. But in this frontal attack upon Labour dogma he was badly defeated. The party simply refused to amend Clause 4.[1]

After much heated debate, a compromise was reached (16th March 1960) between those who would have abolished Clause 4 altogether and those who would have retained it as a sacred cow for worship. A new "Statement of Aims" was drawn up with much sentimental phrasing in the preamble about the "fundamental dignity of man", "the classless society" and "social justice", and with much righteous condemnation of the "selfish, acquisitive doctrines of capitalism" and "the pursuit of material wealth". The party now stands, it said, "for the protection of workers, consumers and all citizens against any exercise of arbitrary power, whether by the State, by private or by public authorities". (They might have added "or by trade unions".) Finally:

> "It is convinced that these social and economic objectives can be achieved only through an expansion of common

[1] C. A. R. Crosland in *The Conservative Enemy*, Jonathan Cape, 1963, blames "the extreme conservatism of the British working-class movement" for this defeat. The assault on Clause 4 was beaten back by an unnatural alliance of the old right wing of the party with the new left—united under the banner of the 1918 constitution.

ownership substantial enough to give the community power over the commanding heights of the economy. Common ownership takes varying forms, including state-owned industries and firms, producer and consumer co-operation, municipal ownership and public participation in private concerns. Recognising that both public and private enterprise have a place in the economy it believes that further extension of common ownership should be decided from time to time in the light of these objectives and according to circumstances with due regard for the view of the workers and consumers concerned."

This Statement of Aims virtually converts the Labour Party from an authoritarian Marxist set-up to the democratic socialism of a mixed economy in which private enterprise can work happily along with public enterprise. The new policy gives Wilson the right to refuse, if he wishes, any further nationalisation beyond iron and steel, water and some road transport. He need not even nationalise all the steel companies: he can pick and choose. The statement gives him freedom to improvise his policy as he goes along in the best empirical tradition of British politics. Instead of nationalising old industries he can create new industries by setting up State-owned enterprises to develop new techniques and skills, as I believe he intends to do in chemical engineering and machine tools. But if he wants private enterprise to play he will have to kill the traditional Labour opposition to profit-making.

In the old days socialists were brought up on the idea that profit-making was immoral. The new socialists will have to learn that profit-making—or the creation of a surplus—is an essential part of efficient enterprise in the private sector and that there is nothing immoral about a profit provided it is not an outrageous one. A lack of growth in profits must be regarded as harmful for the State. The profitability of private enterprise is the hallmark of an efficient economy and as the State under the new socialist régime will be expected to become partners with private enterprise in many joint ventures it should be as keen to make reasonable profits as the capitalist. Indeed, profit-making will have to be encouraged. When the State advances money to private enterprise, it must insist on profitability and a slice of the equity share capital. Hitherto State subsidies have been handed out without an equity cut.

The Labour idea that equity share owners are parasitic and out of date betrays an apalling ignorance of the key mechanism of the private enterprise system. In an advanced industrial state the capitalist system could not exist without the legal device of the risk-bearing share which attracts speculative finance because it takes all the profit or loss. Anthony Crosland in his *Conservative Enemy* tried to write off share ownership as meaningless or unimportant because, he said, the new managers are more anxious about good public and labour relations than about profits. How wrong he is! The only reason why the new managers of the big corporations appear to Crosland as not seeking to maximise company profits as ruthlessly as the old owners did in the past is simply because they find it extremely difficult to do so. They find themselves up against the trade unions who are seeking to maximise wages. They find themselves up against the immobility of labour and the directions of Government departments compelling them to site their factories in areas of high unemployment. And, finally, they find themselves up against the Treasury, which has been damping down domestic demand, cutting profit margins and increasing costs. All the new managers of the big corporations I have known personally have felt the same keen interest in equity shares as the old-style capitalists. They have been just as eager to increase equity earnings and dividends. Some even more so because they have been granted options on blocks of equity shares. It is still a free-enterprise system in which everyone is on the make and pursuing his own private interest and profit. I can assure Anthony Crosland that the private interest and profit of the new managers depend entirely on the growth of the equity share.[1]

Therefore Wilson must not tax company profits to death. If he does he will destroy the mainspring of private enterprise.[2] It was unfortunate that he seemed to commit himself in his Swansea speech in January 1964 to the worn-out theory of a discriminatory profits tax, that is, to a high tax on distributed profits and a low tax on retained profits. This would merely discriminate against the successful, go-ahead companies whose earnings and dividends are on the rise and favour the complacent, slothful directors who sit on idle cash because they are too

[1] For a discussion of the morality of equity share "growth" see page 182 et seq.

[2] A corporation or company tax is discussed in the next section.

lazy or unimaginative to put their funds to useful work. Hoarding is bad for the economy and a discriminatory profits tax would encourage hoarding.

Ever since Wilson made his provocative speech in South Wales the stockbrokers' offices in the City have poured out memoranda showing what horrible effects this two-tier profits tax system would have on share values in the market. This suggests what is likely to happen in the company board rooms if such a discriminatory tax becomes law. More time will be given to the minimisation of discriminatory taxation than to the maximisation of output. Directors will be closeted for days and weeks with their tax accountants and lawyers working out how the extra burdens can be avoided and the lowest possible tax wangled. If they are prevented from declaring the dividends which they think proper, they will take steps to let the shareholders have some other form of profit, for example, a capital repayment (which attracts no tax) or a convertible loan stock convertible into equity shares ten years hence (when the chances of Labour being in power are deemed slight) or the right to subscribe for a new issue of shares at a price greatly below the market. Invariably a way will be found to evade taxation which is considered unfair and oppressive. Wilson may protest that his aim is to "galvanise our sluggish fitful economy", but he will galvanise it in the wrong direction if he imposes a discriminatory profits tax. No private sector in a mixed economy can be expected to produce its best results if the taxes imposed on it hamper and frustrate the most efficient managements and put a twist on the normal pursuit of profit. No enterpreneur is encouraged by having his enterprise more heavily taxed than his laziness. If Labour is seeking the maximum growth possible for the economy, this is not the way to get it.

Harold Wilson may have forgotten what his own socialist advisers said when they signed the memorandum of dissent in the report of the Royal Commission on the Taxation of Profits and Income in 1955. They were then objecting to an immediate uniform rate of profits tax and they added this rider:

> Once capital gains are brought within the scope of taxation the problem takes on an entirely different aspect. For in the long run a private-enterprise economy is likely to function more efficiently if neither higher dividend distributions nor

> the emergence of capital gains is prevented by discriminatory measures. We recommend therefore that after the introduction of the capital gains tax the corporation profits tax[1] should be charged at a uniform rate on the whole income of companies.

As Wilson proposes to stiffen up the present capital gains tax there is no reason why he should not return to the excellent advice which Nicholas Kaldor and his colleagues gave on the Royal Commission.

Finally, the Labour Party must accustom itself to the idea that the efficient profit-makers in a mixed economy deserve what may seem to most of us to be enormous incomes. For these successful men are the pillars of the trading State. It is they who energise the export trade and enable the nation to pay its way in the world and secure a surplus on its balance of payments. It is the heads of the great companies drawing princely salaries (like Chambers of I.C.I., an ex-Inland Revenue official) who are often responsible for the most spectacular successes in the export trade. Wilson has got to make these business tycoons feel that they can work happily and profitably in a mixed economy under a Labour Government. In 1945 his predecessors in office made the mistake of believing that Britain could be run by £2,000-a-year salaried men. Very few of the new managers whose praises Anthony Crosland sings are earning as little as £2,000 a year: they are on their road to more stimulating incomes and the possession of sizeable blocks of equity shares of their own and their associated companies. It is when they are rich and making £20,000 a year and keenly interested in the Stock Exchange that they are most likely to make a success of our mixed economy—and earn a surplus in the balance of payments for a Socialist prime minister.

[1] For a discussion of a Corporation Profits Tax see pages 164-5.

SEVENTEEN

# CAN LABOUR SATISFY THE WORKERS?

HAROLD WILSON could also be the first Labour prime minister capable of offering a new deal acceptable to the working class. The trade unions have hinted that they are willing to agree to "wage restraint" in return for certain conditions which a Labour Government—but not a Conservative one—would be able to guarantee. These conditions cover a more equitable taxation of company profits and private capital and a new "charter" for the workers.

"Wage restraint" would have to be a principle observed without a formula. The National Incomes Commission would have to be abandoned. As a piece of administrative machinery it is too complicated, too difficult to work, even if the N.I.C. were to become a politically neutral body.[1] The employers and the trade unions working on a reformed N.E.D.C. together with the new Ministry of Production which Wilson proposes would have to agree upon the percentage rate of growth which they expected of the economy for the year and the T.U.C. would have to advise the individual unions to keep within this percentage in making their wage claims. But it would be understood that the detailed productivity forecasts might vary the percentages allowed for wage increases in the different industries.

In this democratic society the amount of each wage increase must be left to individual bargaining between employers and trade unions in each industry. After all, their wage negotiations in the past have not paid close attention to the index of national productivity or the cost of living. They have depended on the exercise of reasonableness and common sense and, fortunately, the British people have a large measure of both. The trade unions know perfectly well that the nation cannot go on paying itself more money for the goods and services it produces than it gathers in by way of their disposal. If reasonableness breaks down we may have to set up industrial courts with the authority of judicial courts, as Ray Gunter suggested recently in *Socialist*

[1] For a discussion of the administrative impracticability of an incomes policy see page 126 et seq.

*Commentary*. But to make sure that reason and common sense do prevail, the Government should be represented at each important wage negotiation, that is, hold a watching brief, so that the public point of view can be presented and the plain facts of economic life kept in mind. Above all, the Government as the largest employer of labour, should practise what it preaches.

The trouble in the past has been not that wages have risen too fast, but productivity too slowly. This has been due partly to the restrictive practices of the trade unions, but mainly to the stupidity or sloth of managements who have failed to apply new industrial techniques in time. Nepotism and the "old school tie" are still largely responsible for the amateur approach of most industrial boards. Both managements and men have got to change their ways. Restrictive practices would have to go and managements and unions with the help of the reformed N.E.D.C. would have to agree upon a concerted plan to raise output and productivity by every device of automation.

Next, the trade unions will want a Government guarantee that in the division of the national income the shares taken between wages and profits will not be altered at the expense of wages, that is to say, that profits will not go up merely because wages are held down. Since the war the wages share of the national income has kept around 42%.[1] (It was 39·9% in 1938.) The profits share has actually been falling since the spurt it received at the time of the Korean war boom. But too much importance must not be attached to these statistical calculations. The percentage share of salaries, for example, tends to go up as more and more classes of workers (like shopkeepers) come out of the manual into the "white-collar" class. The wages share may in consequence be lower although individual wage earnings have gone up. The profits share is bound to rise or fall with changes in the economic climate.

The simplest way for the Government to give the workers an assurance that restraint on their part will not mean extra profit for the employers is to bring in a company or corporation tax and raise it if profits start climbing at a higher rate than the gross national product. Suppose that the G.N.P. rose at 4% (and wages at 3½%) and suppose that company profits rose at 7½% in the same period, the extra 3½% would then attract a higher corporation tax. This corporation tax would

[1] See table on page 68.

be in lieu of income tax and profits tax. As companies are now paying 38¾% of their profits in income tax and 15% in profits tax, making a total of 53¾%, I would suggest that the corporation tax should start at around 50% for a special reason.

British companies have not been paying as high a proportion of the cost of social security as their competitors on the Continent. In West Germany and France, for example, the employer pays about 1*s.* 9*d.* out of the total wage of between 5*s.* 1*d.* and 5*s.* 7*d.* per hour to meet the cost of social security.[1] In our country the comparative figure is 8*d.* The British employers have therefore been tempted to hoard labour and to be wasteful in its use. This has been one of the main causes of our bad productivity record. To make employers keener to use labour more economically and scientifically I suggest that they should be made to pay a contribution towards, say, family allowances which now fall directly on the budget. Selwyn Lloyd proposed a pay-roll tax which was so light (4/- per employee per week) as to be farcical. But a contribution towards family allowances should be stiff enough to be felt.

The use of a corporation tax as an instrument of social justice between employers and workers may disappoint some trade unionists who have been brought up to believe that dividends are the capitalist's "take-home" pay packet and that only a differential dividend tax—taking away any dividend increase in excess of the wage increase—will put the two sides on an equality basis. But these dissidents will have to learn a little more about business economics. They will have to appreciate that there are taxation measures which produce greater equity but reduce efficiency. A differential dividend tax would operate unfairly towards young, growing or recovering companies which, having had a lean dividend-less time, are just beginning to build up reserves and distribute to their shareholders a fair reward for their risk-taking. A differential dividend tax would would be positively harmful to the economy and its incidence so unfair as to cause a flight of business capital from Britain.

There remains the awkward question of private as opposed to company taxation. The workers must be convinced that the individual tax system is fair—that there is an equitable distribution between direct and indirect taxation and that the possessors of capital are not more lightly treated than the

[1] Figures of the French National Institute of Statistics and Economic Studies.

possessors of income. On the first they can be satisfied, for the weight is on the side of direct taxation,[1] but not on the second, for the owners of capital are too lightly treated. All that they pay is the estate duty on dying and a notional capital gains tax while they live. The estate duty is certainly very heavy on large fortunes—going up to 80% at the top—but is largely voluntary because it can be avoided by gifts and trusts.[2] A capital gains tax limited to six months for securities and three years for land is obviously not designed to tax continuing capital appreciation. All the speculator need do is to wait a day over six months before selling his shares and a day over three years before selling his land in order to go scot-free. The time-limit makes it farcical as a tax on continuing capital growth. *The Economist* commented: "This will be the costliest exercise to collect an exiguous revenue in the history of our tax administration. . . . This is not in its present form a tax that deserves serious fiscal attention."

James Callaghan has proposed a wealth tax similar to the very stiff one in Sweden which is a small annual tax, ranging from 0·8% to 1·8% on the whole of an individual's capital assessment (including houses, land, jewellery, motor-cars and boats but not pictures, books or works of art), together with a capital gains tax which up to two years is the same as income tax. (After five years nil.) But Sweden is a bad example. Its wealth tax only brings in about £16 million out of direct taxation of £560 million, which indicates that in spite of the fact that the total tax assessment must not exceed 80% of an individual's net income, the very rich have felt obliged to leave the country.

My own tentative suggestion is that the individual taxpayer, not the company paying the corporation tax, should be asked to make a return of capital as well as income and pay, say, 5% on its annual *increment*, thus avoiding the necessity of a capital gains tax which always has a distorting effect upon the capital market. I would estimate that a 5% tax on the annual increment of the individual taxpayer would bring in around £200

[1] 1963-64 direct taxation took £3,990 million and indirect taxation £2,900 million.

[2] If the donor lives five years after the gift it is tax free. The Finance Act 1960 provided for a reduction of 15% in the principal value of the property if the donor dies in the third year, 30% in the fourth and 60% in the fifth.

million. But the expense of collection would be high and the more thoroughly efficient—and expensive—the collection were to be, the greater the risk of seeing the large fortunes emigrate to countries where the rich are more welcome.

Various estimates have been made by Oxford statisticians of the amount of private wealth in this country. James Callaghan seemed to think it was only £20,000 million. It is much more likely to be well over £60,000 million. The Revenue in their latest annual report estimated private wealth in 1962 at £58,196 million (owned as to 58% by ten million men and as to 42% by eight-and-a-half million women) against £54,222 million in 1961. The number of people in the millionaire class —with incomes over £100,000 a year—went up by five to a total of ninety-two. The Labour party makes great play of the fact that 2% of the population still own 50% of the national wealth. We would all agree that there are too many property millionaires but provided we close the avenues for what I call "instant" money-making and take political power away from the minority clique of finance-capitalists there is no harm to the community in having a tiny percentage of very wealthy individuals. They can do a lot of good in the promotion of speculative new enterprises which the State could not possibly undertake.

Finally, if the workers are to co-operate whole-heartedly in a new deal on the lines I have suggested they will have to be given a new charter, a new social status. No longer can working men be regarded as second-class citizens liable to be dismissed on a day's notice. They must receive service contracts like salaried employees, entitling them on the termination of the contract to, say, a week's pay for every year's service. This has just been agreed to, as I write, (June 1964) by the Ford Motor Company at Dagenham, which has often set the pace in the advance of workers' pay and working conditions.[1]

Redundancy, which is constantly being brought on by automation, is the nightmare of the trade unions, and the

[1] The Ford "Workers Protection Charter" provides for (*a*) one week's pay for each year of service for redundant workers. [Special merit money will be paid so that craftsmen leaving after, say, twenty years service could pick up at least £320.] (*b*) A week's notice over and above anything agreed in the Contracts of Employment Act. (*c*) Full consultation with the unions when redundancy is anticipated. (*d*) A general "last-in-first-out" policy. (*e*) A pledge to maintain security of employment "by all reasonable means" before sackings are agreed.

feeling of insecurity it generates will never be removed until the Government has an adequate scheme for compensation, re-training, re-settlement and re-housing. (At the moment there is no national scheme for training the adult worker whose job has disappeared through some automation process.) In the factories workers must be consulted more by the management and treated as partners in the enterprise. Of course, managements must retain control over policy, but in the day-to-day administration of the factory the management and its labour force should co-operate through joint committees and these joint committees should include the shop stewards. This problem of industrial relations is largely a psychological one and labour officers should study the science of human behaviour more seriously.

At the same time, a better opportunity must be given to the workers to raise their social status through education. Out of the great education debate now raging a better chance for the clever boys of the working class to receive higher education in university or technical college is obviously going to come. But let us not stop at that. Teaching by means of television (Harold Wilson's "University of the Air") must be pushed forward.

Education apart, the system of apprenticeships needs modernisation. There is much to be said for the French system which puts apprenticeship on an industry basis, each industry setting up committees responsible for the pay and instruction of the trainees. At present about two-thirds of the boys leaving school at fifteen enter no apprenticeship course at all. Working-class ambitions must be fostered. The Coal Board has set a good example with its "ladder plan". Every worker should be made to feel that if he has the will and ability he can end up on the management or at the board room table if he likes it that way.

My conviction is that given a fair system of taxation of company profits and of private wealth—one which is "seen to be fair"—and given a new social status in an industrial charter, the mass of workers would gladly give up their restrictive practices and co-operate in applying a policy not of wage restraint but of what Frank Cousins calls "planned wages". If with these reforms, the trade unions still refused to co-operate, then their days would be numbered. As Ray Gunter has said: "The trade unions are not eternal. They will exist just as long as they are relevant to the times in which they seek to exist."

EIGHTEEN

# SECURING A STAKE IN THE COUNTRY

HOW TO MAKE people who possess no capital feel that they have a stake in the country is an awkward political problem. As long as they suspect that the nation is being run in the interests of the finance-capitalists—the 2% of the population who own half the wealth of the nation—they will always feel alienated and at times incensed.

The Labour attempt to bring about a wider distribution of capital through nationalisation was futile. Their whole socialisation programme tended to make the rich richer. And it brought no uplift in the worker's status. It was merely a change, as I have said, in management—and that of a peculiarly bureaucratic type. The railway workers, for example, must feel, if Dr. Beeching has his way, that far from having a stake in the country, they do not even have a stake in the railways.

Labour should realise that a wider distribution of capital cannot be secured by nationalisation (which makes the rich more liquid) or by heavy discriminating taxation (which would merely drive the rich abroad) or by confiscation (which is rightly impossible in a democratic state). It can only be done by making poor people less poor and giving the mass of wage and salary earners a better chance to acquire some capital.

In the *Westminster Bank Review* for February 1964, Alan Day suggested a new way for solving this problem. This was to issue for public subscription "national equity" bonds paying a gradually increasing dividend related to the rise in the gross national product. As the G.N.P. is expressed in monetary terms, the dividend would rise not only with the growth of the economy but with price-inflation. Thus, if real growth in any one year were 4% and if price-inflation were to account for an extra 3% in monetary terms, the dividend would increase in the following year by 7%. The idea seems to me absurd. The subscriber to a "national equity" bond, far from feeling that he had a stake in the economic success of the country, would probably feel that he had a stake in the economic collapse of the country. For his dividend would go up the more the nation failed to secure growth without inflation. The honest worker would feel disgusted; the more cynical would regard it as a racket and would jump at the chance of adding to the inflationary part of the national dividend by supporting frivolous wage claims. National morality would take a severe beating. Indeed, an immoral government would undoubtedly seize the opportunity to buy votes by promising higher and higher dividends on these "national equity" bonds. We would quickly descend to a state of dear money, shady finance and raging inflation worse than that of any spendthrift Latin-American republic.

Now there is much to be said for an honest attempt to give the workers a chance to accumulate savings—that is, capital—and to make that capital grow, but Alan Day's bright idea is really drawing a red herring across the track. A better plan is for the State to make use of the unit trust technique and invite public subscriptions to a genuine equity fund comprising shares of the leading, and growing, companies in every industry in the country. Unit trusts, as I have said, have caught the fancy of the middle class and the rate of public saving through this medium has risen in the last five years from about £20 million to £80 million a year. An even faster growth could be achieved if employers were to give facilities to their work-people for unit trust savings when the weekly pay-packets are handed out.

In my opinion the Government should run its own unit trusts and make available their 5*s.* or 1*s.* units at the Post Office counters like other forms of savings documents. This was an idea I put out in *The Spectator* as long ago as 9th May 1958 but it was not taken up until Douglas Jay seized hold of it in 1962-63. I hope it will become part of the savings policy of the next Labour Government.

Having now had some experience of the management of unit trust portfolios,[1] I have come to the conclusion that the State should issue two distinct trusts—under one management, of course, to save working expenses—which would appeal not only to workers seeking to accumulate some capital but to those who already possess some capital and want to see it grow.

First, I suggest an Estate Duties Unit Trust—EDUT to distinguish it from EDITH the private-enterprise Estate Duties Investment Trust—which would invite public subscriptions

[1] I am the investment adviser of three.

to a unit trust formed to hold the best shares taken over from private estates under the Estate Duties. The trust would be highly selective. It would inform the trustees of the deceased estate which shares it was prepared to take over and which shares it would refuse at any price. Picking the best—it would take non-quoted securities as well as quoted—it would offer a unique "growth" portfolio which, I am sure, would be immensely popular with the investing public.

Secondly, I propose a State Participation Unit Trust (SPUT), which would invite public subscription to a unit trust formed, like any other, to buy holdings in the equities of well-managed private-enterprise companies quoted on the market. It was at one time the policy of the Labour party to acquire holdings in the industrial leaders of the private sector by purchases in the open market. I am not sure whether this policy has been officially dropped or shelved, but I am putting my plan forward, not to further back-door socialisation, but simply as a means of giving the uninvested public "a stake in the country" which it would otherwise find difficult to acquire. The equity portfolio of this trust would be carefully selected for "growth" and profit record. Provided the management is in expert investment hands—independent of the Treasury and the Civil Service—I am sure that it would be a raging success. I assume that the investment managers of the state pension funds would be empowered to invest in the units of both Government unit trusts.

I am not oblivious of the fact that these State unit trusts would give a socialist government an increasing stake in private enterprise—the Treasury being the registered holder of the shares—but I am not trying to promote socialism by the back door. The advantage I stress is that they would encourage small savings and would allow any subscriber with even a modest accumulation of capital to feel that he had a stake in the country when he bought his first £100 of units.

There is, of course, another way in which the worker can acquire capital wealth. That is by profit-sharing, but I hold this to be objectionable. It creates a new privileged clique within the working class at a time when we are all anxious to abolish privilege. It we take the total working population at 24,000,000, I would guess that not much more than one-third would be eligible for direct company profit-sharing. First, we have to exclude all those working for the central Government and its armed forces, its nationalised industries and its public boards, all those working for local services, such as police, public health and education, and all those professional, scientific, domestic and welfare services which have no equity profits to share out. Secondly, we must omit the vast amount of enterprise which the Government classes as self-employment —farmers, shopkeepers, one-man trades, private family businesses—not to mention the huge public companies engaged in financial services such as insurance, banking, hire purchase and property, where participation in equity profits is either not practicable or not easily workable. We are left with a small minority of companies engaged in manufacturing and trading which can effectively offer their workers a share in the equity.[1] Why should this minority be privileged above the vast working mass? Take the case of the great Imperial Chemical Industries. This company has a profit-sharing scheme which requires 22% of the total amount paid out in dividends or interest on all forms of the company's stock (after making certain deductions) to be handed over to trustees who use it to buy ordinary shares for the workers at current market prices. Recently the bonus has come to about £10 million a year divided among about 100,000 employees at so much net per £1 of salary. Why should I.C.I. chemical workers be privileged to receive £10 million and not others? No doubt some managements feel sincerely that their employees are entitled to a share in the profits. Others may believe that it gives their employees such a sweetener as will make any future offer of nationalisation

[1] There are fifty or more different schemes for employee-shareholding or profit-sharing (See *The Challenge of Employee Shareholding* by Dr. George Copeman, Batsford; Business publications (London), 1958). Employee shareholding can be arranged in five ways; (i) by buying shares at the market price out of monies accruing to workers from a profit-sharing scheme (as in the case of I.C.I. and Courtaulds); (ii) by employee savings, matched by a company contribution, being invested in ordinary shares (as in the case of G.E.C.); (iii) by employee savings being invested in the capital of the company at par but with ordinary share dividend rights (as in the case of Rolls-Royce, Lucas and Tootal); (iv) by employee savings being invested in preference or loan stocks with a right of conversion into ordinary stock (as in the case of Birfield Industries); (v) by creating a special class of employee shares acquired out of workers' savings—with or without a contribution from the company—which are entitled to dividends matching or even exceeding the dividend rate on the ordinary share capital, thus giving the prospect of great capital gain (as in the case of Rugby Portland Cement). Many variations of these types exist.

by Labour seem a bitter pill. But it is obvious that these profit-sharing schemes must create bitterness and a sense of injustice in the fraternity of workers.

I am therefore against any form of profit-sharing. It will only aggravate, not relieve, the social stresses in the economy. It will increase the unequal distribution of wealth and extend privilege to select managements and workers. Carried to its logical conclusion, employee profit-sharing leads to syndicalism in which management and labour gang up to exploit the consumer.

Equally I am opposed to stock options granted to managing executives. These are usually bribes to induce the ablest, if greediest, managers to stay with a company that feels itself dependent on managers' brains but the practice is regarded by both workers and shareholders as an affront to the principle of fair shares. Besides, the managers are already being well looked after with "top hat" pensions schemes, expense accounts and motor-cars. And they can easily finance the purchase of a block of their company equity shares at market prices if they want to.

The fact that the "executive option" is widespread in the United States, where management ability is rated high, is no reason why it would be encouraged in this country. To get rich quickly is an American tradition and the executive heads of their great corporations expect to be given the chance to acquire great blocks of shares and become dollar millionaires on their way up the management ladder. The President cannot call upon the services of a McNamara (or expect him to be released by General Motors) unless he is rich enough already to work for the Government virtually for nothing. But there are different customs in this country and public opinion would not accept the creation of so many new millionaires each year as American industry proliferates. The recent crop of property millionaires was sufficient unto our day.

NINETEEN

# THE ANACHRONISM OF A MONEYED RULING CLIQUE

IT WAS UNFORTUNATE that some of the 1945 Labour leaders in their stumbling approach to a wages policy got themselves identified in the eyes of the workers with the old ruling clique. One might have expected it of Attlee (Haileybury) or Dalton (Eton) or Cripps (Winchester), but who would have thought that Ernest Bevin would behave like an old Harrovian? The explanation of this tragedy is that the traditions of the old ruling class live on in the services—especially the Civil Service—and that the Labour Ministers, bowed down by their appalling problems, became faint in the arms of the policy-making higher civil servants in the Treasury.

As we all know, the Establishment is recruited from the public schools and there is no doubt that higher education of this privileged and expensive sort turns out some extremely able men. As John Vaizey wrote in 1959:[1] "They (the public schools) do throw up leaders in most important spheres. . . . All the High Court judges but one; all the bishops but one; almost all Tory M.P.s and a third of the Labour M.P.s; the whole Cabinet—the list could go on." The public schools still monopolise more than half the places at Oxford and Cambridge and "Oxbridge" still monopolises the higher places in the Civil Service.'[2] The cleverest among them who have won their "firsts" in P.P.E. (Politics, Philosophy and Economics) go into the Treasury because it is the top policy-making department. As soon as they are inside they might just have well have entered a monastery for all the contact they keep thereafter with the outer world. They will be trapped

[1] John Vaizey in *The Establishment: A Symposium*, ed. Hugh Thomas, Anthony Blond, 1959. This should be read for Dr. Thomas Balogh's penetrating essay on the Treasury and Whitehall: "The Apotheosis of the Dilettante".

[2] In answer to a parliamentary question in June, 1963, the Financial Secretary to the Treasury produced a table showing that in the open competitions for Assistant Principal level over the past ten years Oxford secured 194 places, Cambridge 149. London 35 and seven red-brick universities only 15.

like monks for the rest of their unnatural lives. They will have taken their monastic vows in what is virtually a religious seminary devoted to the ancient mystique of the £ sterling. They will perform the solemn monetary ceremonials of deflation required by the mystique oblivious of the psychological effect which their depressing spells have upon the frail human managers and workers in the business world outside. The reason why they behave in this extraordinary esoteric manner is that in their public schools and universities they imbibed the outlook and attitudes of their friends who were destined by family or wealth to become members of the ruling class. No better example of this identity between civil servant and ruling clique could be found than Sir Frank Lee who rose from Brentwood Secondary School via Cambridge to the Colonial Office and finally the Treasury where he advised Selwyn Lloyd on the crudest anti-proletarian policies of the Conservative epoch.[1] His public-school predecessors could not have been more ardent in the service of finance-capitalism.

It has been said: "Whoever is in office, the Whigs are in power." This was a profound remark which showed that someone had done his historical research. The present ruling class can trace their origin back to 1660, when the great property owners and the rich City merchants got together in common funk of the revolutionary radicalism of the lower classes which the Civil War incited. They brought Charles II back to the throne because they feared the socialism preached by the Levellers and the Agitators in the army. After the revolution of 1688 this ruling clique split into two camps—Whigs and Tories—the Whigs representing the landed aristocrats and new merchant capitalists, the Tories the lesser but more numerous country gentry. Gradually a new capitalism emerged out of the agrarian revolution in the eighteenth century and out of the industrial revolution in the nineteenth, but the country gentry remained the backbone of the Tories. As the workers became politically more conscious, the ruling class had to drop its cynicism (its pocket boroughs, etc.) and make concessions to democratic reform. Hence the great Reform Bills of the Victorian epoch. But there was no surrender of power

[1] I am aware that the organisation of the Treasury underwent a massive change last year under the new régime of Sir William Armstrong, and I am prepared to believe that the deflationary madness of the Selwyn Lloyd epoch will never be repeated.

on the part of the ruling class. Whigs and Tories, Liberals and Conservatives went on dishing out social reform but clinging to power and were not seriously challenged until the rise of the Labour party.

This old ruling class was steeped in the mercantile tradition, the modern version of which I call finance-capitalism. Britain became rich and great in the mercantile era and although the industrial revolution of the nineteenth century created a new group of capitalists, these neo-industrialists stayed largely in the provinces and allowed the finance-capitalists in the City, the inheritors of mercantilism, to remain in the seats of political power. This explains why London has been allowed to dominate for so long the economic and political life of the country. This also explains why the ruling class was so determined to put the country back on to gold in 1925 at an over-valued rate for sterling. A fixed gold £ was deemed essential to enable British finance-capitalism to extend its investments overseas and to carry on its international finance-banking with its ancillary insurance and broking business.

Historically, British industry has been largely developed and financed in the provinces by businessmen exploiting some new industrial technique and putting back their hard-won earnings into their business. It is only since the war that the industrial demand for capital has been far too great to be financed locally out of profits, so that the big industrialists have been forced to come more and more to the capital market in the City. This has given the finance-capitalists a further opportunity to extend their money power. The curious feature of this development is that it is in the old Whig, not Tory, tradition, but with the decline of the Liberal party the Tories have stepped into the shoes of their old rivals. The Tory country "gentry", of course, have had to be quietened with farm subsidies to condition them to accept the cheap food imports of the new mercantilism, but the Tory ruling clique, now Benthamite in character, has become a Whiggish money power.

This transformation has been assisted by the present dominance of the old Etonian in the Tory coterie. The old Etonian as a rule has inherited wealth and his mind is trained to think in terms of money; that is to say, how to make money out of the manipulation and exploitation of money in banking, insurance, trading and bulk commodity and metal dealing.

He will not want to know how to make money out of manufacturing or wholesaling or retailing. His father may have been a business tycoon—a shop-keeper or merchant—but the son will look down upon the business of making or trading things and will drift naturally into politics or the City. In the City he will go into the merchant banks, the discount market, Lloyd's, the Stock Exchange and the investment world. With the exception of Catto, all the Governors of the Bank of England within my working lifetime have been old Etonians. When the Labour party made an inquiry a few years ago, it found that 44 our of 148 directors of the joint stock banks, 46 out of 149 directors of the large insurance companies and 35 out of 107 directors of big City firms were all old Etonians.

If you look into the industrial directorships of the old Etonian and other public school directors of the key financial institutions—the Bank of England, the joint stock banks, the merchant banks and the insurance companies—you will find that they interlock and cover "the commanding heights of the economy". By this network of directorships the money power of the present ruling class pervades the whole of British industry.

In my investment work I have always tried to avoid the shares of companies which have a public school banker in the chair because I know that the money influence will be predominant and that the scientist-technician, on whom our industrial future depends, will be conspicuous by his absence from the board. But I have found this simple investment rule almost impossible to follow. The cases where a successful industrial company is managed by an "absolute outsider" with a scientific training, who has never seen the inside of a public school, are so few they would not fill a page of an investment portfolio.

It will now be clear why the public school ruling clique in this country instructed their public school civil servants in the policy-making Treasury to give first priority in their economic management to "hard" money or the strength of sterling, for without it the activities of finance-capitalism would be harmed and restricted. This has meant slowing down the growth of the economy in the interests of the £ and the balance of payments and I do not believe that this has been the right policy for an industrial nation to pursue which has to keep a vast labour force in full employment. It was a policy which made sense in the great mercantile era when London was the financial capital of the world and Britain was a great creditor nation, paying for one-third of its imports by the invisible exports of banking, shipping, insurance, overseas earnings and commodity trading. But after the Second World War it became obvious that if we were to survive as a great industrial and trading power it could only be, as Austin Albu has put it,[1] "by the hard selling of technologically advanced goods in the world markets". The all-important aim is to give top priority not to building up our reserves but to the expansion of our sophisticated trade, to the modernisation of our industrial plant and to the improved productivity of our working people. But the Tory ruling clique could not see it. They could only think in the hard money terms of finance-capitalism. They have been holding back expansion to keep the £ strong. They have been investing overseas when they ought to have been investing in new industrial processes and techniques at home. The Bank of England has been strongly supporting this policy, for it has never refused foreign exchange to a finance-capitalist making a remunerative investment overseas. Certainly this mistaken policy has been ably carried out—the item "interest, profits and dividends" in our "invisible" account has actually been doubled in the last ten years—but it has been done at the cost of abnormally slow growth and the alienation of the working masses.

At the inquiry of the Radcliffe Committee, one of the frank official witnesses was Robert Hall, then economic adviser to the Treasury. Being an Australian, he was free from the taint of old Etonian finance-capitalism and was able to retain a sense of reality in all the monetary moonshine of the Treasury. He was the first to admit that there had been a conflict between the objective of full employment and growth and the objective of hard money. One cannot understand the period after 1951, he told the Committee, without recognising that there had been such a dilemma. Of course there is no dilemma, no clash between finance-capitalism and domestic industry, when the £ is stable. That was the situation in 1962-63 when Maudling was able to increase both public spending and investment because the balance of payment was then showing a good surplus —and perhaps because the dollar was more suspect at that time than the £. But if and when the £ is again threatened, the

[1] *Encounter*, July 1963. See also Shanks's article.

Bank of England will be pressing the Chancellor to crack down on the domestic economy with dear money and credit restriction. The "stop-go-stop" monetary technique was born out of finance-capitalism.

If the nation were to make more profit as a banker than as a manufacturer and merchant trader selling £4,000 million worth of goods to the four quarters of the world, we might begin to join with the Establishment in worshipping the £ as a sacred cow. But there is no comparison between the two. I would estimate the purely banking profit at under £30 million and the total profit of the City institutions at not much over £100 million. To make the £30 or £100 million you employ only a few clerks and top hats in the City: to make the £400 million profit on the export trade you have to employ millions of workers. Certainly the City's earnings are a valuable source of revenue. Certainly the City's activities are very ably carried on and its reputation for fair dealing second to none in the world. Indeed the use of sterling, as I have argued, is due not so much to foreign confidence in the £ as to foreign satisfaction with and respect for these unrivalled services offered by the City institutions. In what other city in the world is a word on the telephone regarded as a bond? But this is no reason why the interests of finance-capitalism should dominate the industrial and trading livelihood of the working masses. A City-based moneyed ruling class is surely an anachronism today.

TWENTY

# THE REVOLUTIONARY CHALLENGE TO SOCIETY

WILL THE REVOLUTIONARY challenge to society die away, as far as this country is concerned, if the next Labour Government satisfies the workers with its "package deal"? By "package deal" I mean an industrial charter offering a new social status and security, a stake in the country by means of a public unit trust, and a fair taxation of profits and capital as a *quid pro quo* for the planning of wages. One cannot be certain. If Wilson makes a mixed economy work with public and private enterprise combining happily together to boost the national output and raise the standard of living his very success will arouse ferocious opposition. The communists will be furious if a democratic mixed economy is proved to be a workable alternative to authoritarian socialism. So will the left wing of the Labour party whose bible is still the Marxian Clause 4.

We must not forget that the revolutionary challenge was merely side-tracked after the war when the Labour Government deluded the people into thinking that a plunge into socialism was being made. It was temporarily forgotten when affluence knocked at the door of working-class homes under the Conservative régime. But affluence led to complacency and complacency allowed the Communist party to infiltrate further into the Labour movement. Aidan Crawley who has made a special study of this subject[1] declares that the Communist party is today increasing its membership and extending its influence among the trade unions. By clever and sometimes dishonest manipulation it has been able to gain control of an important union or two. The first sign of success emerging from a Wilson government would cause it to redouble its efforts. And among Labour's left-wing—the Clause 4 socialists—those who have been left out of the administration would surely begin to intrigue against the leader. We may be sure that the revolutionary challenge to society will not be forgotten.

Curiously enough the challenge does not come only from the Marxists. It derives also from the Catholic Church which has

[1] See his article in *Encounter*, July 1963.

always blamed economic liberalism or the *laissez faire* capitalist system for the spread of the economic totalitarianism of communism. Its thesis is that the natural human rights and dignities of working people have been cruelly infringed by exploiting entrepreneurs who treated labour as a market commodity—to be hired at the cheapest rate—and then grabbed all the profit. Hence, they say, the provocative maldistribution of wealth on this side of the Iron Curtain—two-thirds of the people living in poverty while the other third luxuriates in wealth. Communism owes its origin and existence simply to the violent (and non-Christian) reaction of one class of people to the injustices perpetrated against them by another class.

The chief exponent of this thesis in Britain is the Reverend John Francis Maxwell, the director of the Catholic Social Guild in the diocese of Southwark. He submitted a lengthy memorandum on it to the Jenkins Committee on company law. He argued that there were three serious "moral evils" in the existing system of capitalism; first, the maldistribution of the benefits which derive from the ownership of property; second, the under-consumption of employees during the boom period of the business cycle leading to distress in the downward phase; third, the absence of any limitation of the dividends payable to equity shareholders. As far as Great Britain is concerned we have pretty well eradicated the second evil by ironing out the severe trade cycles of the pre-war period. But the others remain as a necessary effect of the operation of existing company law.

The Reverend Maxwell makes great play of the enormous gains which have accured to ordinary shareholders in "growth" companies which have financed themselves largely by ploughing back their earnings. He gives the following examples, the figures of which have been calculated for him by Moodies Services Ltd.

| | *Date of investment of £100* | *Value of this investment on 30.3.62* £ |
|---|---|---|
| Associated British Foods | Dec. 1935 | 7,167 |
| Beecham Group | Jan. 1928 | 12,757 |
| Grattan Warehouses | June 1935 | 19,549 |
| Marks & Spencers | June 1928 | 37,672 |
| United Drapery | June 1927 | 6,352 |

This is an appetising table for the avaricious but I could have given him an even better example of capital appreciation. The *Financial Times* has stated that an investment of £2,000 in General Motors in 1916 would have become worth £1,428,000 in 1955. And at the present rate of growth an investment in International Business Machines will probably turn out even better than one in General Motors.

The presentation of these fabulous examples of capital growth is calculated to shock the puritanical as well as whet the appetitite of the greedy. I can imagine the cries of indignation from the left wing if the Labour party introduces the public unit trust and advertises the future capital gain which a subscriber might expect. Is this not lowering the moral standards of the country, introducing a gamblers' state and going back to the Macmillan cry of "we've never had it so good"? The reply is No. The answer is to have a sense of proportion. The fabulous capital gains are the exceptions to the investment rule. The rule is for the average man's portfolio of equity shares to hold its own against the fall in the value of money but not much more. It is only the investment experts who can manipulate a fund to any great advantage. If an economy is growing at the rate of 4% per annum in real terms it will only be the cleverly managed portfolio which will beat the index. The Church of England Commissioners were wise to call in experts for the management of the Church portfolio, for by increasing their equity share stake at judicious moments they have more than doubled the value of their investment. The Church did not consider this accretion of wealth from the equity share markets as ungodly or immoral. Nor would a Labour Government regard it as immoral for the State pension fund to invest in equities and make a "killing" for the pensioners.

But this is not answering the Reverend Maxwell's contention that it is against the "moral law" that the equity share should be allowed to take the jack-pot. The Catholic Church, he says, has always taught that the rate of return on invested money should be "a moderate rate" or "a fair rate" or "a rate prevailing in the open market". It has never tolerated the idea that there should be an unlimited return. As for the element of risk, this varies in different sorts of industry. In certain jobs, he argues, the risk of accident or injury is greater than in others, so the man employed to do dangerous work rightly deserves extra "danger money". But he does not get unlimited danger money. Similarly an investor who risks his money in a risky business venture deserves extra danger money by way of a higher dividend but this does not entitle him to unlimited dividends. A lot of the extra economic growth which is now taking place, he says, is due neither to hard-working labour nor to risk-taking capital, but to the free intelligent application of mathematics, science and technology. Neither the philosophy of *laissez faire* capitalism nor the philosophy of communism can rightly claim to be the magic which causes economic growth. So the Catholic doctrine is that increases in productivity and growth of capital need to be subject to the natural moral law if they are to confer real benefits on the whole of society. Moral law, they say, demands a limitation of the rate of return on equity capital, the surplus going to the State.

It might be argued that this attack on *laissez faire* capitalism is somewhat out of date. *Laissez faire* is already half-dead. Even in America limitation of the rate of return to equity capital has been enforced for many years in the public utility industry where the rates charged for gas and electricity have to be approved by a Federal Commission. Of course, public utilities are very different from the normal risk-taking private enterprise and I suspect that the private sector of our economy would utterly refuse to work on a fixed scale of returns based on an official assessment of the different risks involved. At one time I toyed with the idea that a variable fixed return might be practicable for tax purposes if applied with great flexibility but I have come to the conclusion that it would cause the private sector to come virtually to a stop. New enterprise would be killed stone dead. Innovation and invention would be stifled. The economy would slow down and British industry would not be able to compete abroad and earn our living. One might fix a fair rate of return for a particular industry and then find that a newcomer in that industry who had an important new technological innovation to exploit was taking an enormous risk in setting up in competition with the established vested interests and therefore deserved a much higher return on his capital. The legal device of the equity share which takes all the profit or loss is the hub of the private enterprise system—the magic which makes it work. Without it we could not secure the finance of risky enterprise. The whole complicated machinery of the capital market—whereby the savings of the people are channelled via the insurance companies and pension funds into the pockets of the capital spenders via issues on the Stock Exchange—would break down if the equity share were tampered with.

Of course, the next Labour Government could not allow this huge volume of savings to flow through the capital market into the pockets of the capital spenders without any direction at all. The present semi-*laissez faire* has led to a lot of investment of the wrong sort. Labour would want to favour investment which makes use of the latest labour-saving techniques and is most likely to increase our exports and cut down our imports of manufactures. For this reason the Labour party pamphlet "Signpost for the Sixties" emphatically declared that "a greater control over the investment policies of pension funds and private insurance companies" would be required. It is said that Harold Wilson favours the setting-up of some form of central committee to co-ordinate and direct institutional investment policy. Seeing that last year the new money invested by the pension funds and insurance companies accounted for about half the total amount of personal savings and for about half the total investment in the private sector excluding housing it is certain that this last stronghold of *laissez faire* will be brought under subjection when Labour regains power.

Given some State direction of private investment there is not much left of *laissez-faire* for the Catholic Church to attack. We will then have, in effect, a controlled form of capitalism working inside a democratic mixed economy in which public and private enterprise have their allotted spheres of operation. If the private sector makes an excessive profit it will be checked by the new corporation tax which the Labour party proposes. And with the new charter for the workers, which, I hope, will soon be introduced, it cannot be said that this controlled form of capitalism in the private sector is likely to trample upon "the natural rights" of the working people.

Looking back I have seen and felt the stress and industrial conflict in the 'twenties, the depression and mass unemployment in the 'thirties, the frustration and disillusionment over the socialist failure in the late 'forties and the pathological cynicism under Tory rule in the affluent 'fifties and early 'sixties—and I am not surprised that the working class retain their sense of alienation. Now we must wait to see what kind of society will develop if we are given the shock of a long-awaited change of government. Happily in this country it is traditional to make an empirical approach to politics. We do not sit comfortably on uncompromising ideologies. The mixed economy of public and private enterprise is still an experiment and we will not know whether it will succeed until we have tried it for another span. If Harold Wilson leads a government which wins the confidence of both managements and men, which understands the technical application of science not only to industry but to industrial relations, which knows how to pursue a policy of economic growth without looking over its shoulder all the time at the state of the gold reserves, he will have a good chance of making a success of it. It may be that with a greater understanding of human behaviour and of the techniques of a sane financial system our society may achieve an integration which has so far been denied us. As I said in the beginning, only primitive societies are at one because they have one binding moral code. But in a sophisticated society such as ours it is not impossible to achieve an integration by a mutual understanding of our differences—our different approaches to work, to leisure, to morals, to culture. If we tried to conform to one rigid economic and political pattern—capitalism, socialism, communism—we highly individualistic, if not eccentric, Anglo-Saxons and Celts would soon be at loggerheads. So let us extend the great experiment of what is, in effect, an advanced industrial democracy applying the more enlightened and rational disciplines of both socialism and capitalism in fine disregard of any known ideology. As far as these islands are concerned this may be the answer to the revolutionary challenge to society.

There are two conditions for success. Politically the Government must be drawn not from the old moneyed ruling clique of the capital but from every class and from every province and from every accent. Economically we must have a humane financial policy; we must put men before money. Finally, we must disestablish the Establishment. But I advise the next prime minister to "play it cool". This is a serious moment—perhaps a turning-point in the history of our nation which, in spite of its shortcomings, is still the most decent liberal society on earth.

# BIBLIOGRAPHY


Balogh, T., *Planning for Progress* Fabian Tract 346, 1963. See also his chapter "The Apotheosis of the Dilettante" in *The Establishment*. (See below, Hugh Thomas.)

Barna, T., *Investment and Growth Policies in British Industrial Firms* (National Institute of Economic and Social Research, occasional papers No. XX, Cambridge University Press, 1962).

Bates, James and Reid, G. L., "Supplementary Labour Costs and Their Effect on Wage Bills" (*Three Banks Review*, September, 1962).

Bevan, Aneurin, *In Place of Fear* (Heinemann, 1952).

Beveridge, Lord, *Full Employment in a Free Society* (George, Allen and Unwin 1944).

Blackaby, F. T., *The Recent Performance of the British Economy* (British Association for the Advancement of Science, March, 1963, page 489).

Boothby, Lord, *My Yesterday, Your Tomorrow* (Hutchinson, 1962).

Burn, Duncan, "Why Investment has Fallen" (*Lloyds Bank Review*, April 1963).

Busschen, W. J., *Gold and International Liquidity* (South African Institute of International Affairs, 1961).

Clark, Colin, *Growthmanship* (Institute of Economic Affairs, 1961).

Clarke, William, *The City's Invisible Earnings* (Institute of Economic Affairs, 1958).

Conan, A. R., "The Status of the Key Currencies" (Westminster Bank Review, May 1962); "The £ and the $ in the 1960's"; "The Impact of Post-war Capital Movements"; "The Unsolved Balance of Payments Problem" (Westminster Banks Reviews, May, August and November 1963).

Clay, Sir Henry, *The Post-war Unemployment Problem* (Macmillan, 1929).

—— *Lord Norman* (Macmillan, 1957).

Copeman, G., *Employee Shareholding* (Batsford, 1958).

Crosland, C. A. R., *The Conservative Enemy* (Jonathan Cape, 1962).

—— *Britain's Economic Problem* (Jonathan Cape, 1953).

Crossman, R. H. S. and others, *New Fabian Essays* (Turnstile Press, 1952).

—— *Labour in the Affluent Society*, Fabian Tract 325, 1960.

Dalton, Hugh, *Practical Socialism for Britain* (George Routledge, 1935).

—— *High Tide and After: Memoirs, 1945-1960* (Muller, 1962).

Day, A. C. L., *Outline of Monetary Economics* (Oxford Clarendon Press, 1957) "A New Stake in the Country" (*Westminster Bank Review*, February, 1964).

Deane, P. and Cole, W. A., *British Economic Growth*, 1688-1959 (Cambridge University Press, 1962).

Dicks-Mireaux, L. A. and Shepherd, J. R., (1962) "The Wages Structure and Some Implications for Incomes Policy", *National Institute Economic Review*, No. 22, November 1962, p. 38.

Dow, J. C. R. *The Management of the British Economy, 1945-60* (Cambridge University Press, 1964).

—— "Fiscal Policy and Monetary Policy as Instruments of Economic Control" (*Westminster Bank Review*, May, August and November, 1960).

(See also his evidence before the Radcliffe Committee.)

Einzig, Paul, *The Euro-dollar System: Practice and Theory of International Interest Rates* (Macmillan, 1964).

Ferris, Paul, *The City* (Gollancz, 1960).

Fisher, Irving, *The Stock Market Crash and After* (Macmillan, New York, 1930).

Flanders, A., *The Fawley Productivity Agreements* (Faber & Faber, 1964).

Galbraith, J. K., *Economic Development in Perspective* (Havard University Press, 1962).

—— *The Affluent Society* (Hamish Hamilton, 1958).

Gaitskell, Hugh, "The Sterling Area", *International Affairs*, vol. 28, no. 2, April 1952.

Hannington, Wal, *The Problem of the Distressed Areas* (Left Book Club—Gollancz, 1937).

Hall, Sir Robert, "Reflections on the Practical Application of Economics", *Economic Journal*, vol. 69, No. 276, December 1959.

Harrod, Sir Roy, *Towards a Dynamic Economics: Some Recent Developments of Economic Theory and their Application to Policy* (Macmillan, 1948).

Harrod, Sir Roy, "Changes in the Industrial Structure of Britain" (*Lloyds Bank Review*, January 1963).
—— *The Life of John Maynard Keynes* (Macmillan, 1951).
—— *The British Economy* (McGraw-Hill, N.Y., 1963).
—— "Incomes Policy—State of Play" (*Three Banks Review*, March 1964).
—— "The Keynesians" article in *Encounter*, January 1964.
Henderson, Sir Hubert, "The Anglo-American Financial Agreement" (*Bulletin of the Oxford Institute of Statistics*, vol. 8, No. 1, January, 1946).
—— *"The Inter-war Years" and other papers: A Selection from the Writings of Hubert Douglas Henderson*, ed. H. Clay (Oxford, Clarendon Press).
Ilersic, A. R., *The Taxation of Capital Gains* (Staples Press, 1962).
Jasay, A. E., *The Working of the Radcliffe Monetary System* (Oxford Economic Papers, N.S., vol. 12, No. 2, June 1960).
—— "Paying Ourselves More Money" (*Westminster Bank Review*, May 1962).
Jay, Douglas, *The Socialist Case* (Faber and Faber, 1937).
—— *Socialism in the New Society* (Longmans, 1961).
Kaldor, N., *An Expenditure Tax* (George Allen and Unwin, 1955).
(See also his evidence before the Radcliffe Committee.)
Keynes, Lord (J. M. Keynes), *A Tract on Monetary Reform* (Macmillan, 1923).
—— *A Treatise on Money* (Macmillan, 1930).
—— *The General Theory of Employment, Interest and Money* (Macmillan, 1936).
—— *How to Pay for the War: A Radical Plan for the Chancellor of the Exchequer* (Macmillan, 1940).
—— *Essays in Persuasion* (Macmillan, 1931).
Knowles, K. G. J. C., *Wages and Productivity in the British Economy in the Nineteen-Fifties* (Oxford University Press, 1962).
Koestler, Arthur and others, in "Suicide of a Nation", *Encounter*, July 1963.
Labour Party, *Let us Face the Future: A Declaration of Labour Policy for the Consideration of the Nation* (1945); *Towards Equality* (1956); *Industry and Society* (1957); *Signposts for the 'Sixties* (1961); *A Statement of Aims* (1960).
Lekachman, Robert, "J. M. Keynes" (*Encounter*, December 1963).

Little, I. M. D., "Fiscal Policy", *The British Economy in the Nineteen-fifties* (Oxford, Clarendon Press).

Little, I. M. D., "Higgledy Piggledy Growth" (report from *Bulletin of Oxford Institute of Economics and Statistics*, November 1962) (Basil Blackwell).

Mackenzie, Norman and others, *Conviction* (MacGibbon and Kee, 1958).

Macrae, Norman, *Sunshades in October* (George Allen and Unwin, 1963).

Maxwell, Rev. J. F., "Should Christians Press for Revision of Company Law?" (*University of Detroit Law Journal*, vol. 40, No. 1.)

Mennell, W., *Takeover* (Lawrence and Wishart, 1962).

Milbrand, Ralph, *Parliamentary Socialism* (George Allen and Unwin, 1961).

Mitchell, B. R. and Deane, P., *Abstract of British Historical Statistics* (Cambridge University Press, 1962).

Morgan, E. Victor, "Funding Policy and the Gilt-edged Market" (*Lloyds Bank Review*, October 1962).

Mowat, C. L., *Britain Between the Wars*, 1918-1940 (Methuen, 1955).

Neild, R. R., *Pricing and Employment in the Trade Cycle: a study of British Manufacturing Industry* (Cambridge University Press, 1963).

Neild, R. R. and Shirley, E. A., "An Assessment of Forecasts" (*N.I.E.S.R. Economic Review*, No. 15, May 1961).

Paige, D. C., "Economic Growth in the Last Hundred Years" (*N.I.E.S.R. Economic Review*, No. 16, July 1961).

Paish, F. W., "The Economic Problem of the U.K." (*Westminster Bank Review*, August 1962).

Nantevil, Luc De, First Secretary French Embassy, London, "Economic Planning in France" (*District Bank Review*, December 1963).

P.E.P., *Growth in the British Economy* (George Allen and Unwin, 1960).

Ray, G. F., "British Imports of Manufactured Goods", *National Institute Economic Review*, No. 8, March 1960, p. 12; "British Imports of Manufactures", *National Institute Economic Review*, No. 15, May 1961.

Robertson, Sir Dennis, *Growth, Wages, Money* (Marshall Lectures, 1960) (Cambridge University Press).

Robbins, Lord (Lionel Robbins), *The Economic Problem in Peace and War: Some Reflections on Objectives and Mechanisms* (Marshall Lecture) (Macmillan, 1947).

—— *The Balance of Payments* (Stamp Memorial Lecture) (Athlone Press, 1951).

—— "Thoughts on the Crisis" (*Lloyds Bank Review*, N.S., No. 48, April 1958).

Robinson, Austin, "Re-thinking Foreign Trade Policy" (*Three Banks Review*, December 1963).

Robinson, Joan, *Essays in the Theory of Economic Growth* (Macmillan, 1962).

Sargent, J. R., *Out of Stagnation: A Policy for Growth* (Fabian Tract No. 343, 1963).

Sayers, R. S., "The Rate of Interest as a Weapon of Economic Policy", in *Oxford Studies on the Price Mechanism*, ed. T. Wilson and O. W. S. Andrews (Oxford, Clarendon Press).

Scott, M. F. G., "What should be done about the Sterling Area?" (*Bulletin of the Oxford University Institute of Statistics*, vol. 21, No. 4, November 1959,) 1959.

—— *A Study of United Kingdom Imports*, N.I.E.S.R., Economic and Social Studies 20 (Cambridge University Press).

Shanks, Michael, *The Stagnant Society* (Penguin Special, 1963).

Shannon, Ian, *The Economic Functions of Gold* (F. W. Cheshire, Sydney, 1962).

Shonfield, Andrew, *British Economic Policy since the War* (Penguin Special, 1958).

Tew, B. and Henderson, R. F., editors (1959) *Studies in Company Finance: A Symposium on the Economic Analysis and Interpretation of British Company Accounts*, N.I.E.S.R., Economic and Social Studies 17 (Cambridge University Press).

Thomas, Professor Brinley and others, *Commonwealth Perspectives* (Cambridge University Press, 1958).

Thomas, Hugh and others, *The Establishment* (Anthony Blond, 1959).

Titmuss, Richard M., *The Irresponsible Society* (Fabian Tract 323, 1960).

—— *Income Distribution and Social Change* (George Allen and Unwin, 1962).

Tress, R. C., Various titles—*London and Cambridge Economic Bulletin*, N.S., No. 6, June.

Twentieth Century Quarterly, "Money: What they earn and how they spend it", Spring 1964.

Vaizey, John, *Education in a Class Society* (Fabian Tract 342, 1963).

Wilson, Harold, *Purpose in Politics* (Weidenfeld and Nicolson, 1964).

—— *The Relevance of British Socialism* (Weidenfeld and Nicolson, 1964).

Wilson, Thomas, "Inflation and Growth" (*Three Banks Review*, September 1963).

—— *Inflation* (Basil Blackwell, 1961).

Worswick, G. D. N. and Ady, P. H., *The British Economy in the Nineteen-Fifties* (Clarendon Press, Oxford, 1962).

Zweig, Ferdynand, *The Workers in the Affluent Society* (Heinemann, 1961).

*Government Publications*

1. *Committee on Finance and Industry (Macmillan) Report*, Cmnd. 3897, 1931.
2. *United Nations Monetary and Financial Conference, Bretton Woods*, U.S.A. Cmnd. 6546, 1944.
3. *Employment Policy*, Cmnd. 6527, 1944.
4. *Financial agreement between U.S.A. and U.K., 6th December 1945*, Cmnd. 6709, 1945.
5. *Capital Issues Control: Memorandum of Evidence to Capital Issues Committee*, Cmnd. 6645, 1945.
6. *Statement on Personal Incomes, Costs and Prices*, Cmnd. 7321, 1948.
7. *Control of Dividends*. Cmnd. 8318, 1951.
8. *Royal Commission on Taxation of Profits and Incomes*, Cmnd. 9474, 1955.
9. *The Economic Implications of Full Employment*, Cmnd. 9725, 1956.
10. *Report of Tribunal to inquire into allegations that information about the raising of Bank rate was improperly disclosed*, Cmnd. 350, 1958.
11. *Committee on the Working of the Monetary System (Radcliffe) Report*, Cmnd. 827, 1959.
12. *Incomes Policy: The next step*, Cmnd. 1626, February 1962.
13. *National Incomes Commission*, Cmnd. 1844, November, 1962.

14. "*Conditions Favourable to Faster Growth*". *Report of National Economic Development Council;* H.M.S.O., 1963.
15. *Committee of Inquiry on Decimal Currency*, Cmnd. 2145, 1963.
16. *Report of Committee on Turnover Taxation*, H.M.S.O., February 1964.
*Economic Surveys, 1947-1962.*
*Economic Reports, 1962*, etc.
*Economic Trends, Monthly Digest of Statistics, Annual Abstract of Statistics, Financial Statements, National Income and Expenditure of U.K.*
*U.K. Balance of Payments, 1946-1957* and yearly.

*O.E.E.C.*
*The Problem of Rising Prices*, by W. Fellner, Milton Gilbert, Bert Hansen, Richard Kahn, F. Lutz, Pieter de Wolff, O.E.E.C. Paris, 1961.

*Periodicals*
*National Institute of Economic and Social Research Economic Review.*
*London and Cambridge Economic Bulletin* (quarterly in *Times Review of Industry*).
*Bulletin of the Oxford Institute of Economics and Statistics Quarterly* (Basil Blackwell). See "Wage Rounds and Wage Policy" by K. G. J. C. Knowles and D. Robinson, vol. 24, No. 2, 1962 and "Some Concepts Relevant to the Consideration of the Engineering Wage Settlement of November 1963" by the same authors.
*Stock Exchange Statistics—Interest and Dividends and Market Values* published annually by Stock Exchange Council.